sew what! bags

sew what! BAGS

18 PATTERN-FREE PROJECTS
YOU CAN CUSTOMIZE TO FIT YOUR NEEDS

lexie barnes

Storey Publishing

This book is dedicated to all of my teachers — past and present, good and bad — for the valuable lessons they've passed on to me throughout my life.

And to my parents, Ramsay and Gary Klaff, for allowing me to learn things in my own way.

The mission of Storey Publishing is to serve our customers by publishing practical information that encourages personal independence in harmony with the environment.

Edited by Nancy D. Wood and Deborah Balmuth
Art direction, book design, and prop styling by Alethea Morrison
Text production by Liseann Karandisecky

Cover photographs by © Kevin Kennefick, except for back cover, lower left by Mars Vilaubi, and author photo by Claire Folger
Interior photographs by © Kevin Kennefick, except for pages 63, 75 bottom, 76, and 123 by Mars Vilaubi
Decorative pattern illustrations by © Lexie Barnes
How-to illustrations by Christine Erickson

Technical editing by Janet DuBane
Indexed by Nancy D. Wood

Printed in China by SNP Leefung Printers Limited
10 9 8 7 6 5 4 3 2 1

Library of Congress Cataloging-in-Publication Data
Barnes, Lexie.
 Sew what! bags / Lexie Barnes.
   p. cm.
 Includes bibliographical references and index.
 ISBN 978-1-60342-092-1 (hardcover with concealed wire-o : alk. paper)
 1. Tote bags. 2. Handbags. 3. Sewing. I. Title.
TT667.B38 2009
646.4'8—dc22

                    2008042621

ACKNOWLEDGMENTS

I would like to thank the following people:

The lovely folks on the *Sew What! Bags* team for their generosity, kindness, and beautiful work: Pam Art, Deborah Balmuth, Fran Duncan, Amy Greeman, Liseann Karandisecky, Kevin Kennefick, Susan Killam (and Maxwell!), Alethea Morrison, Sheri Riddell, Nancy D. Wood, and the entire Storey Publishing family.

The super sewers: Beth Boggia, Megan Englemann, and Tiffany Jewell for their invaluable contributions toward turning my designs into the projects in this book. And the tests sewers who kindly volunteered to try out all of the projects.

The fabulous people who work for and with the lexie barnes studio: Chris Gondek, Peter Irvine, Michael Kusek, Kim Lambert, April Slone, Amy Wright, all of our interns, and the amazing Jessica Ford.

My friends and colleagues for their support over the years: Kathy and Steve Elkins, Claire Folger, Naira Francis, Gina Frazier, Margot Glass, Holly Kesin, Holly Lawrence, Jeanette Malone, Jillian Moreno, Claudia Moriel, Barbara "Lady B" Neulinger and John Solem, Shannon Okey, Maggie Pace, Jacqueline Sava, Amy R. Singer, and Gina and Austin Wilde.

My family: Patti Barnes, Cheryl and Chuck Carson, Irene Hill, Ben Klaff and Emily Hermant, Adam Scheffler, Linda and Philip Scheffler, the recently departed and dearly missed Natalie "Nannie" Stiefel, and Mary "Mimi" Laing.

And especially: My wonderful husband Cory Barnes and our four sons, Henry, Sebastian, Montgomery, and Calvin, for their boundless patience, encouragement, and enthusiasm. I love you all!

Contents

Introduction

Listen to the Mustn'ts, child, listen to the Don'ts.
Listen to the Shouldn'ts, the Impossibles, the Won'ts.
Listen to the Never Haves, then listen close to me.
Anything can happen, child, Anything can be.

— SHEL SILVERSTEIN

There is nothing like creating something of your very own. The satisfaction born from having an idea — mapping out a plan, tackling the obstacles, and then, at last, holding up the finished product — is immeasurable. This book shows how to use your head, some basic materials, and your own personal style to create fabulous bags again and again — exactly the way you want them, without any patterns, templates, or fussy, stuffy rules to hem you in.

For my part, I can't stand to read instruction manuals, stick strictly to a recipe, or follow the steps exactly as they are written anywhere. If there are too many steps, I'll skip them. If the instructions are too wordy or full of jargon, I'll ignore them and find my own way of doing things. In this book, from the first project to the last, you'll be able to jump right in and start sewing. You'll find simple steps and streamlined projects — fabulous bags you can make on your own to suit your taste, skill level, and style.

A note on fear: It's okay to be afraid to start a project. It's okay to read the book for a while or just look at the pictures until you feel ready to jump in. The trick is that you have to jump in at some point. Like swimming or skydiving or picking up a pencil for the first time — like anything worth doing — you have to start somewhere. Start today. Start now. Don't worry about getting it right or making the perfect bag. It's likely that the first thing you make may not be perfect . . . but you will still treasure it.

In a box somewhere is the very first, very ugly, yellow shirt I had to make for a costume class back in school. It's awful. The experience was terrifying and the class was lousy. But in the end, no matter what it looks like, I made a shirt.

Knowing I could start and finish that project has paved the way for me to create a great many things over the years. If I had caved in to fear on that very first project, I never would have moved on to get where I am today. And if you had asked me back then if I thought I would end up a handbag designer, I would have laughed. The safety net will appear just when you need it. So jump.

 lexie

How to Use This Book

YOU CAN READ ALL OF THE INFORMATIONAL STUFF
up front — or you can jump ahead to the projects and refer
to the guidelines when you need them. You can also start
with the first project and go through them all in order or you
can skip around. Choose your own challenges and make
what you like, when you like. But I do recommend skimming
through everything first, just so you have an idea of where to
find what you need later.

A DESIGN PRINCIPLE

Sewing without a pattern may seem like a scary prospect to some . . . and liberating to others. Personally, I like the freedom and flexibility of pattern-free sewing. I want a bag to work for me, not the other way around.

> *This book is based on the same*
> *simple design principle that I use every day:*
> *Build the bag from the inside out.*

How It Works

THINK BEFORE YOU CUT. Before you begin a project, ask yourself what you'll be carrying in your new bag. You don't need a pattern or template. Just your own eye and an understanding of your needs:

+ *Will this bag be for daily use or for something specific?*
+ *Do you carry a lot of gear with you: phone, keys, gadgets, pens, and notebook?*
+ *Do you want to fish around in your bag to find your phone when it rings? Or would you like a dedicated phone pocket? Where would you like that pocket to be — on the inside of the bag or on the outside, where you can get to it faster?*
+ *Do you need to get to your checkbook easily? Or your lip balm?*
+ *Will you be carrying heavy books or lighter, fragile craft supplies?*
+ *Maybe you want something multipurpose?*

You may be looking to whip up a simple all-purpose tote. Even though you don't need to map out pockets or embellishments yet, you might want to think about the length of the straps.

✦ *Are you 5'1" or are you 5'10"? The answer will affect how long your straps should be, especially if you are lugging something at your side by the handles.*

✦ *Do you like a bag to hang low on your hip? Or do you like it tucked under your arm?*

Experiment with options. Once you know your preferences, you can make notes to save time later. Nothing will be as fixed or precise as working with a pattern, but that doesn't mean you can't get what you want. You'll love watching your own style and preferences evolve.

STRUT YOUR STUFF. Go get everything you plan to carry in your bag. Lay it all out and measure it right on the fabric. Eyeball it, to start. Then, to give yourself something more concrete to work from, grab some graph paper and a pencil. Look at your goodies spread out on the fabric and make a sketch — and I don't mean it has to be pretty. It just needs to be accurate and to scale. (*See* Graph, Paper, Scissors! *on page* 14) By doing this, you can get a good idea of what the shape and size of the bag will be. That's really all the "pattern" you'll need.

In my first year as a designer, I was working on some sketches at my parents' house. I drew the bags in detail, with all of the dimensions "spec'd out." I worked all weekend and I was just in love with the bags I was creating. After preparing my sketches and some notes to send off to a pattern maker, I proudly showed my work to my mother. With a puzzled look on her face, she asked, "You know the dimensions you have there don't match the shapes of those bags, right?" I was horrified! I had measured out sizes that made sense to me and had drawn shapes that pleased me — but I hadn't matched them up together! So I learned that weekend how to put graph paper to good use. And taught myself (okay, Mom helped!) how to create designs that made sense.

GRAPH, PAPER, SCISSORS!

Graph paper is great because it allows you to design to scale. You can easily see and adjust the proportions of what you are design-ing and keep track of your measurements. The kind I like to use is divided into ¼" squares, but it comes in other sizes. Using the ¼-inch-square graph, you can decide what scale you want to use. For instance, if ¼" = 1", each box will represent 1". To draw a bag that is 15" across, you would draw a line that is 15 squares long.

If you want to make a life-size paper cutout, you'll want a 1:1 scale (meaning ¼" = ¼"). For bigger bags, you'll have to tape several sheets together to draw it out. It's fun to cut out your "paper bag" and play with it so you can see how you like it before stitching up the real thing.

HOW DO YOU MEASURE UP? A simple way to make sure your bag fits you well is to take a look at what you already own. Do you have a favorite handbag or backpack? Measure the length of the straps and use that measurement as a standard for your personal fit. Working on the apron or holster in this book? Grab a belt from your closet or an apron from your

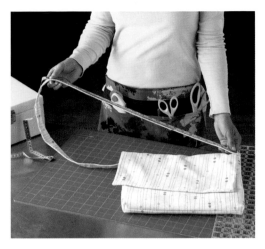

kitchen, and check the length to see how long your waist belt needs to be. Don't forget to add a few inches to that measurement so you can tie it — about 12" to 14" on each side is enough for an average bow.

EASE INTO IT. When planning your pockets and pocket panels, be sure to lay out the objects that will go into them and to measure them carefully. Make the pockets a little shorter than the items you want easier access to (like pens and such) and higher for things that you want to tuck in and protect (like your new camera). For all pockets, you'll want to add ease (a little extra breathing room) to your core measurements. For instance, a pocket for your comb can be pretty flat, but if you're packing a hairbrush, you'll want a pocket with a little more space to allow for the depth. It will be easy to see what you need once everything is laid out in front of you.

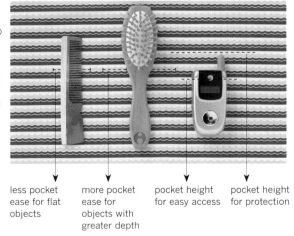

less pocket ease for flat objects

more pocket ease for objects with greater depth

pocket height for easy access

pocket height for protection

Testing 1-2-3

Sometimes, you might want to test out your design before making the final project. It's a good way to try things out while you are developing your design skills. Here are a few ways to see how you're doing.

1. **OH SEW PRETTY.** If you are an experienced sewer, you can make a mock-up bag out of muslin or other inexpensive fabric to test your bag design before making the final version. This can help you save money and time on your final project, so you don't make mistakes on the fabulous imported fabric you just fell in love with!

2. **KNOW WHEN TO FOLD 'EM.** A fun way to test out your design is to map out your bag and then fold your fabric to the size and shape you'd like it to be. But don't cut the fabric yet — this is just a test! Simply pin it together the way you think it should go. For this, I recommend safety pins, rather than straight ones. They'll hold the mock-up together safely so you can play with it without getting pricked by straight pins. This kind of test bag may be a little bulky and it won't be as pretty as the real thing, but you can get a good sense of where you're headed. You can try out pockets, strap lengths, embellishments and other playful options. Once you've patched it together the way you want it to be, make some notes and then get sewing.

muslin bag

pinned bag

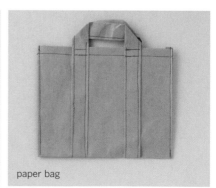

paper bag

3. **THE PAPER CHASE.** Here's an even easier test. I lay out my goodies, draw my sketch on graph paper to get the scale right, then draw or trace the bag onto plain paper and cut out the pieces. Then I stitch up the paper! Sometimes, I even skip the sewing: I just staple and/or tape the pieces together. To this day, I use this test method. Sometimes I'll reduce the scale to make a miniature version of the bag so it will be more manageable. Often, I use my kids' construction paper or scrap paper from my recycling bin. It's cheap, easy, and quick. You can tell right away if you've got a good design or if you need to go back to the drawing board.

Inspiration

A terrific tool that I highly recommend is an idea board or notebook. In my studio, I dedicate an entire wall to this. At home, I keep binders full of ideas and inspirations. In the binders, I categorize the pages so I can find what I'm looking for later.

There are great ideas all around you. Rip out pictures from magazines, find swatches or paint chips, anything that strikes your fancy. Keep them up on your board for inspiration. When you are working, look up at it. See what shapes you picked. Which colors are you most into these days? Have you been dying to play with polka dots? Even if you think you don't have a personal style yet — you probably do. You just need to let it surface!

If you are going through magazines, you can use a technique I call the "flip and rip." I go through the magazine really quickly, just flipping through it. When something catches my eye — a color, pattern, shape, vibe, or what-have-you — I rip out the page. Those are the images that hit me first and fast. I don't stop to ask myself what I like in the picture, I just rip it out and keep flipping. That page goes up on my board (or in a notebook) until I use the inspiration or I grow tired of the image. Every few weeks, I like to strip the board and put up new ideas for inspiration. I tend to file the old images away, but you don't have to. The best ideas will stick with you.

SEWING TOOLS

Here's what you need to get started. The basic tools are easy to find at your local fabric store. You can order online, but be sure to ask any questions you have and check the return policies *before* you make your purchase. There are a few things you don't want to skimp on, like needles, shears, and of course, your sewing machine. If you find a deal that looks too good to be true, it very well may be. Talk to the shop clerk or owner and get the skinny. Buyer beware = sewer prepared!

Assumptions

We assume that you have a basic sewing machine and know how to use it. With so many different sewing machines out there, we can't give specific instructions on how to operate yours. Refer to your manual if you need to. If you don't have a manual, you can find one online (*see* Resources) or invite a friend or family member to help get you started. The rest is just practice.

Once you can thread your machine and fill the bobbin, you can pick up your scrap fabric and practice some stitching. Most of the projects in this book don't require zippers, but if you'd like to add them, you'll need a zipper foot. If you want to add buttons to anything you are making, your machine may have a buttonhole attachment. Get familiar with your machine, your manual, and how all of your attachments work. All of the projects in chapter 2 are made from scraps, so once you are comfortable with the basics, you're good to go.

Your Sewing Kit

In addition to your sewing machine, you will want to have the following items on hand:

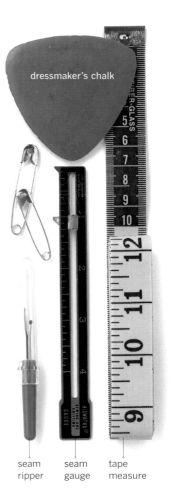

dressmaker's chalk

+ *good pair of sharp shears used only for cutting fabric*
+ *pair of pinking shears (which make a zigzag edge) to finish seams*
+ *rotary cutter, mat, and cutting ruler for long straight lines*
+ *small pair of scissors for clipping and trimming*
+ *straight pins and a pincushion*
+ *magnet (a great tool for picking up spilled pins)*
+ *tape measure, sewing ruler, or yardstick; seam gauge*
+ *variety of hand-sewing needles*
+ *variety of sewing-machine needles*
+ *seam ripper*
+ *safety pins*
+ *dressmaker's chalk or disappearing fabric markers*
+ *steam iron and ironing board*
+ *point turner (see Cutting Corners on page 21)*
+ *weights: paperweights, cans, or any small items with some heft to hold down pieces of fabric while you are pinning and cutting*

seam ripper

seam gauge

tape measure

NEEDLES AND PINS. Sewing-machine needles can get dull after only a few hours, so check them regularly for burrs and dull points, and always have spares available. Who wants to run out to the store for replacements while in the middle of a project? They come in a variety of sizes and types. Smaller needles are better for lightweight fabrics, and larger needles should be used on heavier fabrics like denim or canvas. You can start out with a size 12 and go up or down from there. Pick up a package of assorted sizes to keep around. You can check your sewing machine manual for guidance on how to choose the right needles or you can ask someone at your neighborhood fabric shop.

Long straight pins with very big heads and very slender shafts are the best for most fabrics. Pins with glass heads are easier to see. Try not to leave pins in fabrics for weeks — you'll be amazed at how fast some nonrust pins will rust! A good pincushion or two makes it easy to grab a pin when you need one — or try a magnetic pin holder.

SCISSORS, SCHMISSORS. Technically, you call them scissors when the length is 6" or less and the finger holes are the same size. Shears are usually 7" to 12" long, with one larger finger hole (to fit two or more fingers). Whether you are using scissors or shears, it is important that they are comfortable and fit your hand. You'll want something that feels good to you, is easy to open and close, and isn't too heavy. To keep fabric shears sharp, do not use them to cut paper, cardboard, aluminum foil, or hair!

CUTTING CORNERS

+ Although building a collection of cutting tools is helpful in the long run, you can actually get by with one pair of shears (a.k.a. scissors), as long as they are very sharp.

+ A tape measure is good for anything you're measuring, except when you're using a rotary cutter. You really need to use the cutter with a mat underneath, and a ruler designed for the task. (*See below*.)

+ A chopstick makes an excellent point turner (for pushing out corners when turning a stitched bag right side out). You can also use the eraser end of a pencil. But I don't recommend a pointed knitting needle; it could poke holes — yikes!

+ If your iron doesn't have a steamer function, you can use a spray bottle and mist your fabric while pressing.

ROTARY CUTTERS AND MATS. A rotary cutter and mat are excellent tools for all your sewing projects. They allow for speedy, tidy cutting and produce a perfectly straight line every time. But it's important to use them carefully. A rotary cutter is a very sharp tool with a round blade that is used to cut fabrics. It should only be used with a rotary-cutting mat, to protect surfaces from being damaged, and nonslip rulers designed for use with your rotary cutter and mat. Protect your precious fingers or you'll have to take a long break from your fun projects!

SEAM RIPPER. This small, must-have tool is used to unpick stitches without cutting into fabric. Great for opening seams, cutting off buttons, and taking out basting stitches.

THREAD. Thread comes in a variety of weights and types. Typically, you want to match the fiber content of your thread to your fabric. For the projects in this book, an all-purpose polyester or cotton-wrapped poly thread will do the trick. If you are using different types of fabrics on one project, you should match the thread to the heavier fabric. If you want to match the color of the thread to your bag, go for the dominant color in the print. And if you don't find an exact match, go a shade darker to hide the thread. Lighter colors will pop and be more noticeable. That said, feel free to use thread as a decorative feature. A contrasting thread color is a great way to add spice to an otherwise simple bag. When in doubt, always turn to the staff in your local fabric shop — it's better to ask for help than to suffer the consequences.

CLOSURES. In this book, the bags either self-close (the Tissue Pouch), or have a drawstring (the Ditty Bag and Backpack), a tie closure (the Tool Tote), a zipper (the Zippered Wristlet), or a flap (check any of the messenger bags in chapter 6). But there are plenty of other ways to close a bag. You can use buttons and buttonholes, snaps, buckles, Velcro, hooks, clasps, and so on. If you are looking for a greater challenge, go ahead and modify your bag to add a more complicated closure.

NOT-SO-INVISIBLE MARKERS

Not all marking pencils, pens, and chalk will work on all fabrics. Read the manufacturer's directions and test the marker or chalk on a scrap of fabric before using it on your projects. Make sure the chalk or marker doesn't bleed through or stain your fabric.

FABRIC FACTS

Choosing fabrics is fun and exciting — but it can also be overwhelming. The key is to take your time. Whether you are browsing online or in your local fabric shop, take the time to look at everything. Take it all in. No matter what you are looking for, I urge you to make friends with the shop owners and staff. They know so much and are often your greatest ally in finding the very best materials for your projects. Once you start sewing, you'll be back again and again, so it's nice to get to know the people in your favorite shops.

RIGHT SIDE, WRONG SIDE

The right side of a fabric is the side on which the design or motif is printed. This is what you see on the outside of a bag. The wrong side of the fabric is the back or unprinted side. This is what you see on the inside if your bag is not lined.

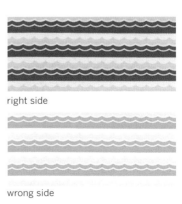

right side

wrong side

Fabric Terminology

SELVAGE. This is the finished edge on either side of the fabric. Selvages are designed to keep the fabric from unraveling. Some are white with printed information about the designer of the fabric, some have little holes where the fabric was attached to the loom, some have fringy edges, and some are just plain.

GRAINLINE. The grainline of the fabric refers to the threads running parallel to the selvage. Sometimes this is called the straight (grain) of the fabric. The crosswise grain runs from selvage to selvage. You generally want to cut out the pieces for your bags along the grainline.

BIAS. The bias runs at a 45-degree angle to the selvage. When you pull fabric along the bias, you will notice that it stretches more in that direction than when you pull on the straight grain. Binding tape is cut along the bias, as stretchiness helps when stitching the tape around corners and curves.

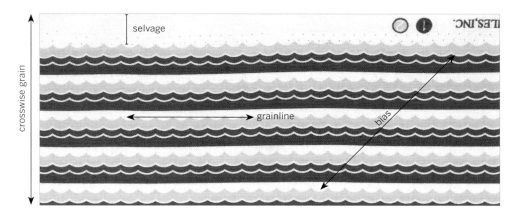

How Much Fabric to Buy

This really depends on what you're making. For the projects in this book, dimensions are listed and the yardage needed to make them. But your needs may vary. When you lay out the intended contents or sketch out the design, you can see how much fabric you're going to need. You can also discuss it with your local fabric store. Tell them what you are planning to make and how big you want it to be and they can help you buy enough fabric. Bring in your sketch and show it to them. I always tend to buy more than I need, just in case. I like to have leftover scraps to use for pockets, trim, or for another project.

UPSIDE-DOWN AND SIDEWAYS

Some printed fabrics are intended to face in a particular direction — for instance, if there are cats, trees, shoes, or other objects that need to be right side up. When using a directional fabric, you may need to adjust how you cut it out, and therefore may need to buy more yardage than listed for a project.

Choosing Fabrics for a Project

When selecting your fabrics, you'll want to consider the kind of bag you are making and what you'll be carrying. For example, if you want to use your bag for heavy items like books or groceries, you will want a stronger, heavier weight fabric like canvas or denim. If you are making a lingerie bag, you can use a delicate, lightweight fabric. Just keep that in mind and when in doubt, go to your local fabric shop to ask if the project and materials are a good fit. For the projects in this book, we used primarily cotton, canvas, linen, and denim. Muslin is good for testing, and sometimes a lightweight flannel works well for lining.

canvas

cotton

denim

flannel

linen

MATCHMAKER, MATCHMAKER

When you are choosing fabric for your bag, be sure to think about how you'll use the bag. There are no hard-and-fast rules, but use common sense. If you plan to carry heavy, bulky items like groceries or books, you'll want a sturdy, durable fabric that can take the weight. If you are making a laundry sack, you'll probably want to use a fabric that can be tossed into the washing machine and dryer along with your clothes.

The same thing applies to the handles and straps. It's great to mix and match fabrics, but you should make sure the fabrics are compatible. If you are using denim for a tool tote, you won't want to use lightweight cotton on the handles — they won't be strong enough. And if your tools are sharp or pointy, be extra sure that the fabric you choose for the pockets is tightly woven and able to withstand use over time.

CANVAS. This fabric is made from a variety of sources, including cotton, linen, jute, or hemp. The term is used to indicate a heavy, tightly woven fabric. Canvas is a great fabric for bags that you'll use to carry heavier loads, like books. It's strong and sturdy, and available in a wide variety of colors, prints, and weights.

The DJ Bag on page 115 is made of canvas and denim.

COTTON. Made from a natural fiber derived from the cotton plant, cotton fabric is available in a wide variety of weights and textures. Basic quilting fabrics are usually 100% cotton and that's what you'll find on bolts at your local quilting or fabric shop. There are countless colors and prints from which to choose and you'll fall in love with browsing through them. Most of the projects in this book have been made entirely from cotton or they have cotton for pockets or trim.

DENIM. This cotton fabric is most commonly used for blue jeans. Once primarily available in indigo, it can now be found in many colors and even some prints. It's an excellent choice for most bags, due to its sturdy but pliable nature. It's easily laundered and can really take a beating.

The Eyeglasses Case on page 51 is lined with flannel to protect the lenses from scratches.

FLANNEL. A light- to medium-weight fabric, flannel is typically made from cotton, a cotton blend, or wool. Flannel is very soft and warm, commonly used to make bed sheets and plaid shirts. Flannel makes a nice lining for bags that might hold something fragile, such as your glasses or an MP3 player.

LINEN. A natural fiber derived from flax, linen is a strong, lightweight fabric that is available in many wonderful colors. While its beauty will dazzle you, it does have some drawbacks. It tends to wrinkle (though you can usually hand- or machine-wash it), you'll have to iron it well, and it can be pricey. That said, linen is a great choice for most of these projects and a lovely way to dress up any bag.

Linen is an excellent choice for dressing up small projects like the Tissue Pouch on page 57.

MUSLIN. This inexpensive fabric is commonly used to make test versions of projects. When you are trying something new, you might consider a first "draft" made out of muslin. Chances are, it will save you money — not to mention grief over the loss of a beloved vintage remnant you've been waiting to use!

Combining Fabrics

I am a big believer in mix and match. You can use different fabrics together and achieve some really cool looks. But it's a good idea to make sure the fabrics are a suitable match — check care instructions and be sure to preshrink both fabrics. The general rule of thumb is to wash and press your fabric before

getting to work. Washing it allows the fabric to shrink — something you don't want happening *after* you make your bag! In most cases, the fabric will look and feel better after washing, too. Wash it according to the fabric manufacturer's instructions (usually found on the bolt end when you buy the fabric) and then press it with your trusty iron.

OTHER ESSENTIALS

While you can make the simplest bag with no lining or closures, you may want to branch out at some point. Adding a lining your bag increases its durability and enhances the look. Interfacing is another way to add longevity and structure. Or maybe you just want to add some color and flair. See chapter 2 for more information on how to incorporate these items.

Lining

Lining is the fabric sewn to the inside of your bag — a great way to strengthen it, give it more shape, add color or texture, and give it a more finished look. Essentially, you make a second bag of the same size and slip it inside the main bag (wrong sides together), fold under the top edges, and machine-stitch or hand-sew the two together. (For details on how this is done, look at the DJ Bag on page 115.) Some of the projects in this book are lined and some are not. It's really up to you. If you are not lining your bag, I recommend using a zigzag stitch (*see pages* 36 *and* 40) to keep your raw edges from fraying.

GET A GRIP!

It's a huge bummer to have your straps rip out, especially when you're out and about and your bag is full! So when you're mapping out your bags, always think about what you'll be carrying in them. You'll want to be sure your straps and handles can take the load. It's a good idea to choose heavier weight fabric for tote straps and to reinforce where they attach to the bag with a box stitch (*see page* 43). A little forethought will work wonders.

Interfacing

Interfacing is a layer of special material you can add to the wrong side of your fabric for extra support and structure. It comes in a variety of weights and in two styles: fusible (iron-on) or sew-in. The projects in this book do not require interfacing, but if you want to try it, just follow the manufacturer's instructions. I recommend fusible interfacing for beginners; just be sure the sticky side is facing the fabric or you'll get adhesive all over your iron.

Batting

Batting is cotton or man-made material used for padding, filling, or quilting. Batting is available in a variety of weights (or "lofts") and materials. You can use cotton, polyester, cotton-poly blends, or wool. If you want to add padding to your bag (between the outer bag and the lining), this is a good way to go (*see page* 136). If you aren't sure which type or loft you'll need, ask your local fabric or quilting store for guidance.

Embellishments

I tend to keep my bag designs pretty clean, but there are a million ways to add your own personal touch to the projects in this book. Here are a few suggestions for you:

APPLIQUÉ. A design that is sewn (or glued) onto your project. The possibilities here are endless, since you can make your own or buy manufactured designs at many stores.

BUTTONS. Can be used as a closure on your bag — but don't limit yourself! Buttons can also be used to add a decorative touch to your projects.

BIAS TAPE. These strips of fabric, primarily used for binding raw edges, are cut on the bias. Bias tape is also great for adding structure, reinforcing edges and pockets, and showing off compartments of your bag. Pre-folded bias tape is available at most fabric stores, in single-fold or double-fold, and in a variety of widths and colors.

You can also make your own bias tape (*see page* 47) by measuring, folding, and pressing strips of fabric cut on the bias. Or you can feed strips of fabric into a bias-tape maker, which folds and presses the strips into "tape" that is one quarter of their original width. Bias-tape makers come in a few different sizes and are available in fabric stores.

EMBROIDERY. A stitched design on your project, embroidery can be accomplished by hand or by using a special machine. (*See* Resources *for some suggestions.*)

FABRIC MARKERS, PENS, AND PAINT. If you want to draw or paint designs onto your bag, you can find a wide array of choices at your local craft or hobby store.

PATCHES. You can make your own or find fun options at fabric and notions stores. Sew-on and iron-on varieties are available.

RIBBON. Use ribbon for drawstrings or simply for decoration. Choose from an entire rainbow of colors, widths and textures to make your bag sing.

TWILL TAPE. Use it for tie closures, straps, drawstrings, or handles. Twill tape is available in different weights, widths and colors.

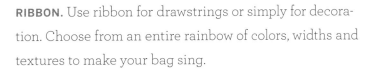

CHAPTER  # Sewing Basics

LIKE EVERYTHING FUN, THERE IS A LOT OF JARGON and mumbo jumbo to learn when you sew. At first, some of the lingo seems daunting. But once you know what the words mean, everything starts to make sense. Don't just smile (even to yourself) and fake it. If you don't know what something means, ask someone or look it up. You'll be surprised to learn that most people are more than happy to share information with you.

HOW TO PIN

TOPSTITCH

STAYSTITCH

EDGESTITCH

PS-1000

PATTERN

INSPIRATION POINTERS

The first thing you need is a comfortable, suitable workspace — a place where you don't have to clear piles of old mail to the side or shove your unfolded laundry down to the floor. It's much easier to get in a creative zone when you aren't distracted by clutter. While you probably don't have an entire room to devote to your sewing, it's best if you can find a dedicated spot for all of your sewing work.

You'll want a sturdy surface for your sewing machine and a stable, comfy seat. I like chairs that are adjustable, wheeled, and ergonomic. Even if you get a lot of natural light, it's wise to use task lighting to help illuminate your projects up close. It's a good idea to be near your computer (or have enough space to pull out your laptop) so you can look up unfamiliar terms, search for tutorials, shop for fabric, or work on your blog.

I can't say enough about getting — and staying — organized. You should give yourself easy access to your fabrics, tools and notions. When you need something, you don't want to stop what you're doing and look all over the place to find it. You don't have to invest a lot of money or time, just use containers that make sense — which means they fit your stuff and your space. By sorting through your fabrics and organizing them, you'll always know where to find them. Thread? Pins? Scissors? Everything — *everything* — needs a place to call home. Keep your supplies in order and you'll be a much happier sewer.

I also highly recommend hanging a bulletin board behind your work table (or somewhere nearby, if you can't fit one behind the desk). Use this "idea board" to post your inspirational findings — or hang tools on it. Pin scraps to it so you remember to use them. Your board can easily turn into your best friend. If you have room, you can put a second, cushy chair nearby so you can take a break and look up at your board or pull out magazines and folders to find new ideas. Find or make a space that works for you!

SKILL LEVELS

While all of the bags in this book are easy to make, some are, well, easier than others. Each of the projects are assigned a skill level, but don't be afraid to jump in where you want to. Sometimes enthusiasm is enough to take you to the next level. Here's how we define skill levels:

NEWBIE. Someone who has either sewn very little or has never sewn at all (but has always wanted to).

PRO. Someone who has made a thing or two and is already comfortable at their sewing machine.

DAREDEVIL. Someone thirsting for challenge and excitement in their crafty endeavors.

SEWING 101

+ **HEM.** A common method of finishing a raw edge by turning it under once or twice and stitching (*see page* 41).
+ **SEAM.** A line of stitching that joins two pieces of fabric (*see page* 38).
+ **SEAM ALLOWANCE.** The area between the raw edge of the fabric and the line of stitching.

WELCOME TO THE MACHINE

Next you need to get to know your sewing machine. Most sewing machines have the same basic stitch settings, which can be changed or adjusted by turning a dial, for instance: stitch length, stitch width, and stitch tension. Be sure to read the section in your manual on how to make these adjustments. Here's a quick review of stitches and what they're good for:

NORMAL STITCH. This stitch is used for most seams. The normal stitch setting is 10–12 stitches per inch (2mm–2.5mm on metric machines).

BASTING STITCH. At 6–8 stitches per inch (3mm–4mm), this is the longest stitch on your sewing machine. Basting stitches are considered temporary and are easily removed. You can also do your basting stitches by hand.

ZIGZAG STITCH. This is used to stitch seams, finish raw edges, and for decoration. Your manual (or a friend) will show you how to control not only how many zigzag stitches per inch, but also the width of the stitch. It's a good idea to test different combinations to get a feel for what the stitch will look like on your fabric. You may need a separate zigzag presser foot with a wider needle opening when using this stitch.

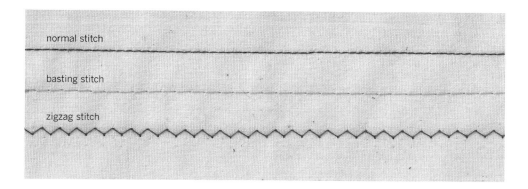

normal stitch

basting stitch

zigzag stitch

The Magic Numbers

It's a good idea to test your stitch length and tension when starting a new project. An easy way to perform the test is to take two scraps of the fabric you'll be using and sew them together. Check (and adjust as needed) the top thread and the bobbin thread of the stitching to make sure the tension and stitch length work well for that fabric and thread. When the stitches meet in the middle (not floating on the top or bottom), pin a piece of paper to the scrap and label it with the stitch length, tension, and kind of thread that you used. This will help when you are making more than one project at a time or have to come back to a project later.

MORE SEWING JARGON

The following machine stitches are not settings on a dial. They describe how stitching is used for a particular purpose. In most cases, a normal stitch setting is used.

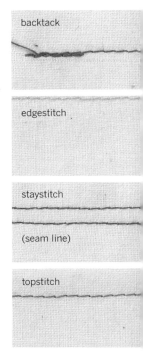

BACKTACK. This term refers to backing up and stitching in the other direction. Backtacking stitches are used mostly at the beginning and end of a line of stitching to prevent it from coming undone. You don't backtack on basting stitches, as they will be pulled out later.

EDGESTITCH. This refers to stitching close to the edge of a fabric piece, on the top of the right side. Edgestitching is done for reinforcement, decoration, or to hold an edge in place.

STAYSTITCH. This is a line of stitches sewn in the seam allowance before the seam is sewn, almost on the seamline. This helps prevent the seam from coming undone when the seam allowance is clipped.

TOPSTITCH. This means that the stitching shows on the "top" or the right side of the fabric. This stitch is usually decorative and sewn in one or more straight parallel lines about ¼" from the fabric's edge.

BEFORE YOU CUT

Once you've washed your fabric, notice which is the right side (outside) of the fabric and which is the wrong side (inside) of the fabric. With right sides together, fold the fabric lengthwise and lay it on a cutting surface. Keep the selvages together and adjust them until there are no bubbles on the folded edge. You may want to pin the selvages in a few places to keep the fabric edges from sliding around.

SEW IT SEAMS

Sewing seams is simple, and basic to the act of sewing. Here's how it's done:

1. Pin two pieces of fabric with right sides together.

    ### HOW TO PIN

    Your pins should be inserted perpendicular to the seam or edge. Position the pinheads to the right so you can easily remove them as you are stitching. You can space the pins as needed; I suggest starting at about 2" apart.

2. Stitch the side you want to sew, ½" from the edge of the fabric. Remove the pins as you go, just before you stitch over them (otherwise, you might break the sewing-machine needle).

    ### HEADS UP!

    For the projects in this book, assume a ½" seam allowance unless the directions call for something different.

right side   seam

wrong side of fabric

backtack

½" seam allowance

3. Backtack at the beginning and end of the seam.

4. Trim the threads at the ends of the seam and remove any remaining pins.

5. On the wrong side of the fabric, open up the seam allowances and press the seam flat. In some cases, directions might call for pressing both seam allowances to one side.

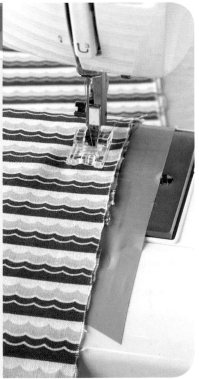

LINE IT UP!

Most sewing machines have marks to the right of the presser foot to help you measure and align your seams. The longest line is usually at ⅝", the seam width most commonly used in commercial patterns. Since we use ½" as our standard, place a strip of tape ½" from the needle hole of your presser foot to keep your seams uniform and straight. As you move the fabric under the needle, line up the edge of the fabric with the tape.

FINISHING RAW EDGES

Along the outer edge of any seam allowance is a raw edge of fabric. This edge will not show, because it'll be inside your bag. But it's possible that the edge could fray or unravel with use or over time. You'll see this for yourself when you prewash the fabric. Some fabrics fray very little, but others unravel quite a bit and you'll end up with a big mess. Whether or how you finish your raw edges is totally your call. Everyone who sews has a favorite method. Try different ones to see what suits you best.

ZIGZAG STITCH. Using the zigzag stitch, sew every raw edge of each seam with the outside point of the stitch at the edge of the fabric.

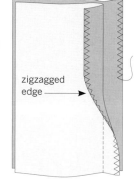

TURNED EDGE. This is just what it sounds like — you turn over the edge and stitch it down. For a neat, accurate line, start with a single line of stitching about ¼" from

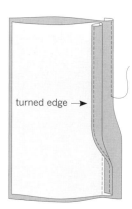

the raw edge. Use this as a guide to press the edge under, and then sew another line of stitching close to the fold. As you gain more practice, you will be able to press without a guide, or even skip the pressing altogether and just fold the edge under as you sew.

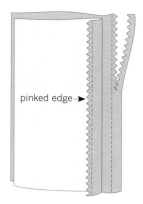

PINKING. Pinking is very easy, and it's worth it to invest in some good quality pinking shears. Just sew a straight line of stitching ¼" from the edge. Then use pinking shears to cut off the outer edge.

FRAY PREVENTER. There are several fray-prevention glues on the market; just follow the directions on the bottle. Be careful or you might end up with glue where you don't want it. It helps to place a piece of heavyweight paper between the seam allowance and the fabric to catch any stray drips.

CUTTING CORNERS

For most of the bags, you will essentially stitch squares of fabric together and turn them right side out. If you are not finishing the seams, you should at least trim them to a narrower, neater width to prevent bulkiness. The corners will need special attention. Clip the fabric diagonally across the corners to get rid of extra material that will get in the way of turning a neat corner.

MAKING A HEM

We think of hems as something on the bottom of a skirt or dress, but any raw edge that is not part of a seam, like the edge of a pocket, will need to be hemmed. The best way to do that is with a double-fold hem. Here's how you make one.

1. Press the raw edge ¼" or ½" to the inside.

2. Press under another ½". If you like, put in a few pins to hold the hem in place while you stitch.

3. Stitch as close to the first fold as you can. With a double-fold hem, the bobbin stitches show on the outside, so choose your thread color accordingly.

MAKING STRAPS

There are essentially two ways to make a strap, a drawstring, or an apron belt, and both methods are fairly similar. You can fold and stitch, or stitch and turn.

Fold and Stitch

The first method is mostly a lot of folding, and is the best bet for making narrow straps. For instance, if you start with a 3"-wide strip of fabric, you will end up with a 1"-wide strap. (*Note:* To make a strap that has a different color fabric on opposite sides, see the Reversible Tote on page 81.)

1. Fold the strip of fabric in half lengthwise, wrong sides together, and press along the fold. Each half will be 1½" wide. Open up the strip, press each side under ½".

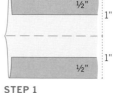

STEP 1

2. Refold the strip with the sides tucked in, and edgestitch along the length of both sides for greater strength.

STEP 2

> **FOR LARGER STRAPS AND BELTS**
>
> For a wider strap that will be used as a belt (*see the* Tool Apron *on page* 129), the method is the same, but turn under the ends ½" before refolding. If the fabric is bulky, trim away excess fabric at the folded corners, then stitch across the folded ends.

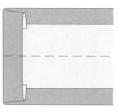

¼"–½" fold on all sides

Stitch and Turn

This method works best for wide straps, like the DJ Bag (*page* 115) and the City Satchel (*page* 121), which start with fabric strips that are 6" to 8" wide.

1. Fold the strips in half lengthwise, right sides together. Stitch the entire length, ½" away from the raw edge.

STEP 1

2. Attach a safety pin securely to one open edge and push it into the opening at one end. Work the safety pin through to the other end, turning the strap right side out as you go.

3. Press the strap flat, and edgestitch along the length of both sides to strengthen the strap.

STEP 3

The Box Stitch

A box stitch is made by stitching a square or rectangular box, and then stitching an "X" inside the box. This stitch is used to secure handles to the body of the bag and is especially useful on larger bags, which will need extra reinforcement for strength.

MAKING POCKETS

Throughout this book, you'll find instructions for three different kinds of pockets: individual pockets, pocket panels, and pleated pockets. All three are found on the Caddy (*see page* 143). To make an individual pocket, start with a rectangle that is about 1" larger than the desired finished size, and do the following:

1. Press under the sides and bottom raw edge ½". It helps to press or trim the corner edges at a bit of an angle so the fabric doesn't stick out on the sides.

STEP 1

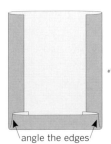

angle the edges

2. Press under the top edge ¼". Press it another ½" and edgestitch along the first fold as shown.

STEP 2

3. With right sides facing out, position and pin the pocket on the front of the bag you're making. Topstitch the sides and bottom of the pocket to attach it, backtacking at the top on both sides. You might want to topstitch around the edge again about ¼" from the first line of stitching.

STEP 3

GET IT STRAIGHT

You'll want to be sure that your pockets are straight, especially if you're using fabric with stripes or other patterns that may accentuate any imperfections. Once you've placed the pocket on the body of the bag, measure the distance from each top pocket corner to the top edge of the bag. These measurements should match. Pin each pocket in place before stitching.

MAKING A CASING

A casing is what you make to hold either a drawstring or elastic. For either one, the casing is made essentially same way. The stitching of the side seams will vary, depending on what you're making (each project will tell you what to do). Often an opening is left on one or both sides, which is where you will insert the drawstring.

The example shown is for a casing that will have an opening for a drawstring on the outside of the bag (the most common casing in this book). Here's what you do:

1. Stitch one side of the bag from bottom to top, but stop within 2½" of the top and backtack. Above it, leave a 1" gap unstitched, then stitch the last 1½", backtacking on both ends.

2. Press the seams open. Stitch down the seam allowance on both sides of the opening. This not only keeps them in place, it will be easier to thread the drawstring through the openings.

3. With the bag inside out, press under the top edge ½". Press under again by the amount needed to accommodate the drawstring or elastic (in this case 1") and edgestitch on the bottom fold. With drawstrings, make the casing about 1" wide, not because you need that much room, but because the gathers will look nicer. When using elastic, make the last fold equal to the width of the elastic plus another ⅛" to give you room to stitch the edge. Edgestitch the bottom fold.

4. Inserting a drawstring into a casing is easy. Just attach a safety pin to one end of the cord and use it to push the cord through the casing.

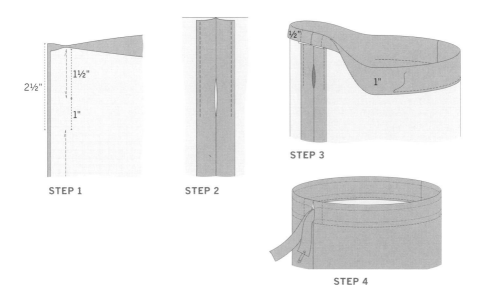

STEP 1

STEP 2

STEP 3

STEP 4

USING BIAS TAPE

What is bias tape? Also called binding, it's a narrow strip of fabric that has been cut on the bias (at a 45-degree angle to the grain) to give it more stretch. Bias tape can be used to reinforce the edges of pockets made from lighter weight fabrics, so the pockets don't sag. It's also a lovely way to add some color and definition to your bags. You can make your own bias tape or buy it prepackaged at your local fabric shop. For the projects in this book, we use double-fold bias tape in either ¼" or ½" widths.

To attach bias tape to a pocket or other raw edge, place the center fold of the bias tape over the top edge of the fabric and pin it in place. Then edgestitch along the bottom edge of the bias tape. Nothin' to it. Here's a little trick, though: When you look closely at the tape, you'll see that the folded sides are not exactly the same width. This is not a manufacturing error, it's intentional. When sewing on bias tape, put the narrower side on the top of the fabric and the wider side in back. When you stitch along the bottom edge (in front), you will automatically catch the back fold with your stitches.

narrower fold

put the slightly narrower fold on top

By the way, if you decide to use bias tape, you won't need to hem the edges of your fabric, so cut your pockets shorter than you would otherwise (in other words, subtract the hem allowance).

Making Your Own

If you have an idea in mind for your bag, but you're just not finding the color you want in a bias tape, the solution is to make it yourself. Creating your own bias tape from a matching or contrasting fabric can be just the touch you need to make your bag truly unique.

1. Decide how wide you want the finished tape to be and multiply by four (the bias fabric strip will be essentially folded in quarters). Cut a strip of fabric on the bias that is the width you need and as long as the pockets you want to bind.

2. The rest is pretty much like making a strap (*see page* 42). Fold and press the strip in half lengthwise. Open up the strip and turn the sides in to almost meet at the pressed center fold. (If you're making ½" or wider tape, the side folds can be less, but should be a minimum of ¼"; adjust the cut width of the fabric accordingly.) As with the commercial bias tape, try to press one folded side slightly wider than the other. Refold and press on the center line and your tape is ready to use.

A bias-tape maker is a nifty tool that simplifies folding the edges of the tape.

Warm-up Projects

A SLIGHT DEPARTURE FROM TRADITIONAL BAGS,

the projects in this chapter fall into the category of "things that also hold stuff." All are simple and some can be made using only scraps of fabric. These fun projects are great for learning the basics and a good opportunity to explore some ideas.

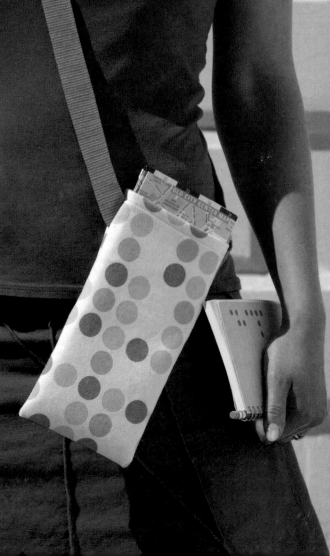

Eyeglasses Case

This is an excellent project for beginners — and for anyone who wants a fabulous case for their specs or shades. Make use of your scraps and get used to customizing right off the bat. Create something totally personal for yourself, or make a gift for someone special.

OUR FINISHED SIZE: 3" × 7"

WHAT YOU'LL NEED

+ 9" square fabric scrap for the exterior of the case

+ 9" square fabric scrap for the lining

+ Sewing supplies (*see page* 18)

WHAT YOU'LL DO

+ Decide your size

+ Cut your fabric

+ Stitch and turn the case

4"

8"

Exterior, cut 2

Lining, cut 2

Exterior, wrong-side out

BEVELED CORNERS

Make It!

1. **DECIDE YOUR SIZE.** Lay your glasses onto fabric to see how much you'll need. A good rule of thumb is to add 2" to the height of the glasses to keep them from falling out. Add just 1" to the width — so the glasses won't slosh around in the case — plus 1" for two ½" seam allowances.

    FABRIC RECOMMENDATION

    It's a good idea to choose a fabric with a bit of weight, especially for the exterior. Fabric that is too thin won't provide much protection for your glasses.

2. **CUT YOUR FABRIC.** Based on your measurements, cut two pieces of fabric for the exterior of the case. Cut two pieces of fabric the same size for the lining.

3. **STITCH THE EXTERIOR.** Pin the exterior pieces with right sides together. Stitch down one side, across the bottom, and up the other side, backtacking at both ends. Trim the seam allowances, clip the corners (*see page* 41), and turn right side out.

    BEVELED CORNERS

    To make angled corners like the ones on our case, stitch diagonally across the bottom corners before trimming, clipping, and turning the case.

4. **STITCH THE LINING.** Pin the lining pieces with right sides together and stitch both sides, leaving the bottom open. Trim excess seam allowance and leave the lining wrong side out.

5. **ASSEMBLE THE PIECES.** Place the exterior case inside the lining, with right sides together. Pin the top edges together and stitch. (If you find the small opening too difficult to stitch with a machine, sew the pieces together by hand.) Trim excess seam allowance.

6. **TURN THE PIECES.** Pull the exterior case through the opening in the bottom of the lining, then turn in the raw edges of the lining, and hand-sew or machine-stitch closed. Tuck the lining into the exterior case.

Other Ideas to Try

BUTTON UP. Want to secure your specs? Try adding a button flap. Here's how:

+ Choose a small- or medium-sized button you love and cut a button tab (a 3" square should do the trick) in addition to the fabric you're cutting for the case.

+ Make your case, following steps 1 through 4.

+ Fold the button tab in half with right sides together and stitch along both sides. Turn the tab right side out and press.

+ Make a buttonhole on the tab that will fit your button. (continued on next page)

Exterior, right side out

Lining, wrong side out

bottom is unstitched

STEP 5

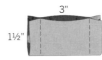

3"

1½"

FOLDING THE BUTTON TAB IN HALF

buttonhole

MAKING THE BUTTONHOLE

**ATTACHING THE
BUTTON TAB**

+ Before moving to step 5, pin the button tab to the exterior of the case, matching the raw edges, and stitch. When placing the exterior case into the lining, the button tab should be sandwiched between the two.

+ Finish up with step 6 (*on page* 53) and then sew on a button. Use small sharp scissors to cut the buttonhole open.

STICK 'EM UP. If you're not big on buttonholes, make the flap as described above, but use Velcro as a fastener instead of a button and buttonhole.

SOFTEN UP. You can also make the case without a lining. Try using a soft flannel, felt, or fleece. These fabrics will offer some extra protection for your glasses and because they don't fray, you can skip the lining altogether. Here's how:

+ When cutting your fabric, only cut two pieces for the exterior.

+ Stitch the long sides and bottom. Clip the corners, trim the seam allowance, and turn right side out.

+ Press under the top edge ½" and topstitch.

1

2

3

4

BITS AND BOBS

Start small! With a little ingenuity and some scrap fabric, you can make cases for all kinds of things. Everything pictured here is easy enough for a beginner to try!

1. diaper case; 2. knitting wristlet;
3. sandwich bag; 4. business card case;
5. lip balm lanyard

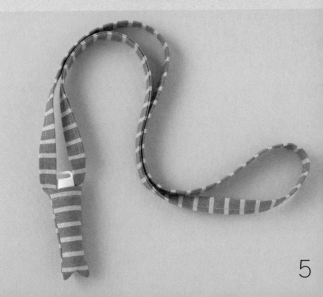

5

Tissue Pouch

SKILL LEVEL
newbie

Don't blow it! Carry your tissues in style. Make one of these cuties to match your new tote bag. Make a dozen for gifts at a bridal shower. This project lets you practice your stitching and learn to make an overlapped opening. Try your hand at appliqué and add some real flair to your pouch. Your tissues have never looked better!

OUR FINISHED SIZE: 3" × 5"

WHAT YOU'LL NEED	WHAT YOU'LL DO
✦ ¼ yard of fabric	✦ Decide your size
✦ Sewing supplies (*see page* 18)	✦ Cut your fabric
	✦ Assemble the pieces
	✦ Stitch the pouch

CUT YOUR FABRIC

4"

Bottom exterior, cut 1

4"

Bottom lining, cut 1

6"

5"

Top, cut 2

6"

Lining

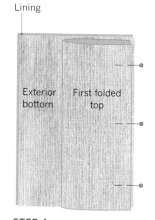

Exterior bottom | First folded top

STEP 4

Make It!

1. **DECIDE YOUR SIZE.** For this project, simply take a pack of travel tissues and measure it. Add 1" to the length and width for seam allowances. To allow for the depth of the packet, add another ½" to both length and width for ease (*see page* 15); otherwise the tissues will be a tight fit.

2. **CUT YOUR FABRIC.** On the wrong side of the fabric, measure, mark, and cut two pieces: one for the bottom exterior and one for the bottom lining. For the folded tops, add another inch to the width of your bottom measurement. Cut two pieces of fabric at that size.

3. **PIN THE PIECES.** Fold each of the top pieces in half lengthwise, wrong sides together. Press them, pin them, and set them aside. Pin together the two bottom pieces, wrong sides together.

4. **ASSEMBLE.** Lay the pinned bottom pieces with the exterior on top and the lining on the bottom. Pin the two folded tops over the bottoms, lining up all outer raw edges. (The folded pieces will overlap in the middle.) If you are using an embellished top piece (like the one in the photo), lay it down first, embellishment side down.

5. **STITCH.** Run a narrow zigzag stitch around the raw edges (this will give the seam a bit of stretch). Trim the excess seam allowance, clip the corners (see page 41), and turn the pouch right side out. And you're done!

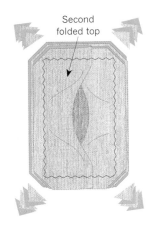

Second folded top

STEP 5

EMBELLISHMENT IDEA

If you want to add a decorative strip, like the one on our pouch, cut a strip of fabric 6" long and about 1" wide. Turn under and press ¼" on the long sides of the strip and edgestitch the strip to one of the folded top pieces before assembling the pouch. Or, use a ribbon that has finished edges, and just edgestitch it on without turning the sides under.

Grocery Bag Tube

SKILL LEVEL
newbie

Don't let recycled grocery bags clutter up your home. Stow them in this sweet and tidy tube instead. Tuck new bags in the top, and pull stored bags out of the bottom. Customize it to fit where you plan to hang it. Do you have a big hook with lots of room below it? Or do you need a shorter tube to tuck into a cabinet? This simple project is practical, makes a cute housewarming gift, and lets you try out using elastic!

OUR FINISHED SIZE: 5" × 26"

WHAT YOU'LL NEED

+ ½ yard of fabric
+ 8" of ribbon or twill tape
+ ½ yard of ¼" elastic
+ Sewing supplies (*see page* 18)

WHAT YOU'LL DO

+ Decide your size
+ Cut the fabric, ribbon, and elastic
+ Make the casing
+ Make and attach the loop
+ Stitch the tube

CUT YOUR FABRIC

11"

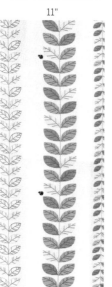

Tube, cut 1

Make It!

1. **DECIDE YOUR SIZE.** This custom job is pretty simple to map out. Use our tube width (11") and decide on the length by measuring where you'll be hanging the tube.

    > **YARDAGE TIP**
    >
    > Save on the amount of fabric you'll need to buy by choosing a nondirectional fabric, like polka dots, and laying the tube on the crosswise grain as we did. This strategy works for a number of the projects in this book.

2. **CUT YOUR FABRIC.** Cut one piece of fabric for your tube and cut two pieces of elastic. Since you need to reach in a little bit to pull out the bags, you can loosely wrap the elastic around your wrist and then add a couple of inches for leeway.

3. **MAKE THE CASING.** To make a casing on the top and bottom of the tube piece, press under the edge ¼", then press again another ½". (The casing needs to be at least ⅛" wider than the elastic to allow for stitching and a bit of wiggle room.) Stitch the two casings.

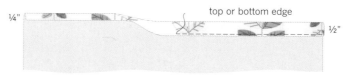

¼"   top or bottom edge   ½"

STEP 3

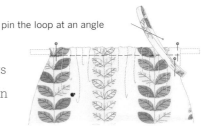

pin the loop at an angle

4. **INSERT THE ELASTIC.** Using a safety pin, thread elastic strips through the top and bottom openings (*see page* 45). Pull them out 1" on each side and pin in place.

5. **ATTACH THE LOOP.** Make a loop with the ribbon and pin it to the right side of fabric about 1" from top of tube at a slight angle.

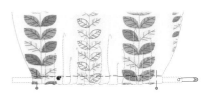

STEPS 4 & 5

6. **FINISH THE TUBE.** With right sides together, fold the tube panel in half lengthwise. Pin and stitch it, backtacking at the ends. You'll be sewing in the ends of the elastic and handle loop when you stitch this seam. Turn the tube right side out.

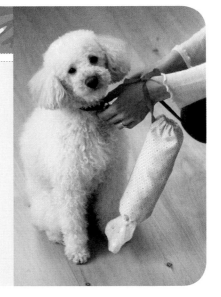

PUPPY LOVE

Make the same tube in a smaller version (ours is 4" x 10"), with two pieces of ribbon instead of a loop. Now you'll have a stylish way to carry baggies when out walking with Fido. Just tie the tube to your wrist or leash and you'll never need to carry an ugly "scooper" again!

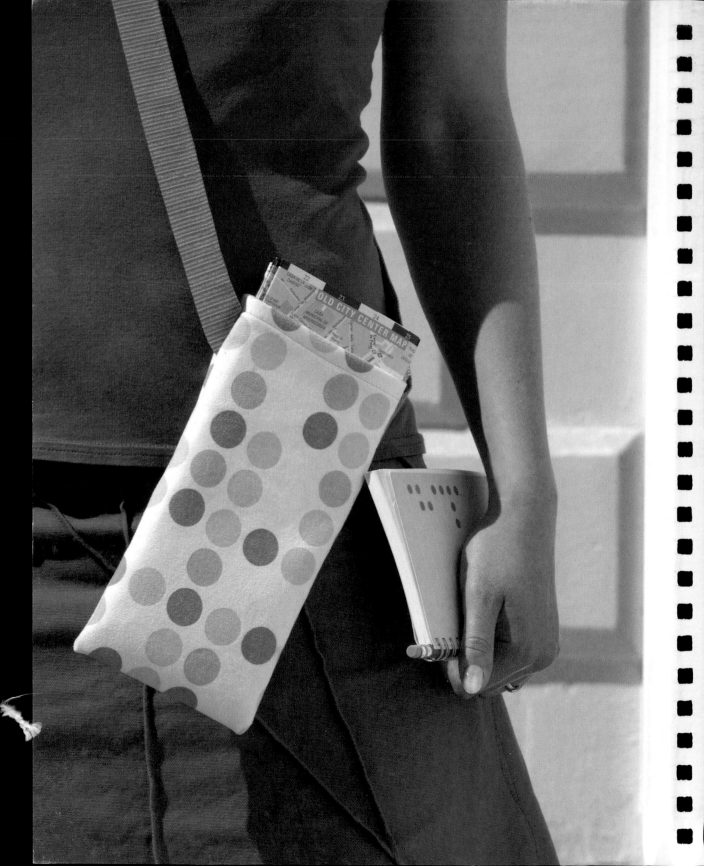

Map Sack

This simple bag can make sightseeing or hiking a little easier. Just tuck in your maps, slip on the bag, and off you go! With this design, you can make bags of countless shapes and sizes. So try this one, then modify it to see what else you can come up with!

OUR FINISHED SIZE: 5" × 8", 44" strap

WHAT YOU'LL NEED

+ ¼ yard of fabric for the bag (ours is made from Ultrasuede)
+ ⅛ yard of fabric for the strap
+ Sewing supplies (*see page* 18)

WHAT YOU'LL DO

+ Decide your size
+ Cut your fabric
+ Stitch the top edges
+ Make and attach the strap
+ Stitch the sides

CUT YOUR FABRIC

3"

6"

Bag, cut 1   18"

Strap,
cut 1   45"

Make It!

1. **DECIDE YOUR SIZE.** Our bag will hold a standard road map, but you might want to check the size of what you plan to carry. Place your map (or whatever) on the wrong side of the fabric to measure how much you'll need to make your bag. It's a good idea to make the bag a little bit shorter than the map (about 2") and a bit wider for ease (*see page* 15). Then you can easily pull the map out and put it back when you're on the go.

2. **CUT YOUR FABRIC.** Follow our measurements, or — based on your own — double the desired length of your bag and add 2" for the hemmed edges. Add 2" to the width for ease and seam allowances. Then cut a 3"-wide strap across the full width of your fabric (which is usually 45").

FOR A LONGER STRAP

Perhaps you are tall, and a 44" finished strap isn't long enough for you. In that case, there are two sensible options: make your strap from 60"-wide fabric; or buy ¼ yard (instead of ⅛ yard) of 45" fabric for the strap, cut two strap pieces, and stitch the ends together. Then you can adjust the length to best fit your needs. (*See page* 110.)

3. **STITCH THE TOP EDGES.** Press under each top edge ½", then repeat for another ½". Pin and edgestitch. Fold the bag in half crosswise with right sides together and pin both sides.

4. **MAKE AND ATTACH THE STRAP.** Make the strap as instructed on page 42. Cut the ends at an angle and insert them between the front and back sides of the bag. The straps need to be inside the bag when you stitch, so they will be on the correct side when you turn the bag right side out. Position and pin the straps just below the folded top edges.

5. **STITCH THE SIDES.** Stitch all the way up the sides, backtacking at the ends. If your fabric is stretchy, you might want to use a narrow zigzag stitch. Otherwise, use a straight stitch and finish the raw edges as you wish (*see page* 39). Trim the seam allowances, turn the bag right side out, and press.

STEP 3

strap ends are inside the bag

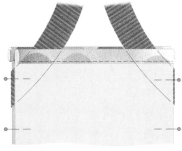

STEP 4

FABRIC IDEA

Ultrasuede is a great fabric choice for almost any bag. It's durable, stain-resistant, and machine-washable. It's pricey, but well worth it!

Zippered Wristlet

A simple, zip-top pouch can hold just about anything. Make a small one for coins, cards, or gadgets. A little bit larger, and you've got a lovely make-up bag. This pouch is great practice for adventurous beginners because the results are so rewarding. Plus, you can get over your fear of zippers!

OUR FINISHED SIZE: 4" × 7½", 13½" strap (optional)

WHAT YOU'LL NEED

- ◆ ½ yard or fabric scraps for the pouch and the lining
- ◆ 8" of ribbon or a fabric scrap for embellishment (optional)
- ◆ ⅛ yard or fabric for the strap (optional)
- ◆ A plastic nylon zipper the length of your pouch
- ◆ Sewing supplies (*see page* 18)

WHAT YOU'LL DO

- ◆ Decide your size
- ◆ Cut your fabric
- ◆ Stitch pieces to the zipper
- ◆ Stitch the sides
- ◆ Turn the pouch and finish the lining
- ◆ Attach the strap (optional)

5"

Exterior, cut 2   8½"

5"

Lining, cut 2   8½"

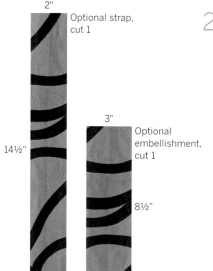

2"

Optional strap,
cut 1

3"

Optional
embellishment,
cut 1

14½"

8½"

Make It!

1. **DECIDE YOUR SIZE.** Follow our dimensions, or make this pouch any size. This is a really fun way to use your scraps. If you're making a pouch to hold something specific, measure the length and width of the items and add an inch or so on all sides for seam allowance and ease (*see page* 15). *Note:* Because this project is challenging, we'll explain it first without a strap. To add the strap, see page 72.

ZIPPER SAVVY

It helps if the length of the pouch matches up with a standard zipper size. You can use a longer zipper and trim it to fit, but be careful sewing over the teeth or you might break the sewing-machine needle.

2. **CUT YOUR FABRIC.** Cut four pieces of fabric the same size (two for the exterior and two for the lining). Cut a strap, and embellishment, if desired.

EMBELLISHMENT IDEA

If you want to add a decorative fabric, like the one on our pouch, cut some fabric the length of the pouch and about 3" wide. Press under the long sides of the strip ¼" or ½" and edgestitch the strip to the right side of one of the exterior pieces, about 1" from what will be the bottom edge (not the zipper edge).

3. **PIN AND STITCH ONE SIDE OF THE ZIPPER.** Lay one piece of exterior fabric right side up and place the zipper, face down, on top of it, lining up the edges. Next, lay a piece of lining fabric on top of zipper, right side facing down. Pin and stitch the pieces together along the zipper edge, close to the teeth. Turn the two fabric pieces down and away from the zipper so the wrong sides are together. Press both edges away from the zipper.

4. **REPEAT ON OTHER SIDE.** Lay the second exterior fabric piece right side up. Place the stitched piece on top, with the zipper and exterior panel facing down. (The exterior pieces will be right sides together, and the first lining piece will be on top.) Line up the edge of the zipper tape at the top. Place the second piece of lining on top, right side facing down, edges lined up. Pin and stitch the pieces together, close to the zipper teeth. Open the zipper a little bit for turning inside out later on.

5. **STITCH THE SIDES.** Open out the pieces with the zipper in the center. The exterior pieces should be right sides together on one side of the zipper, and lining should be right sides together on the other side. If you want to add a strap, refer to Get a Grip! on page 72. Pin and stitch along three sides, leaving the bottom of the lining open. Trim the edges and zipper, if needed.

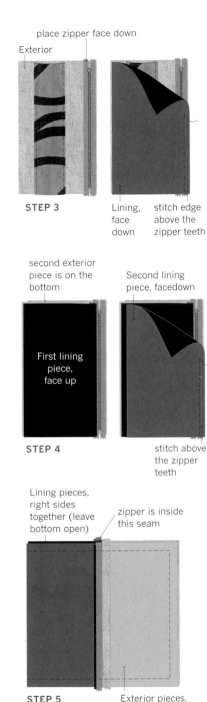

place zipper face down

Exterior

STEP 3

Lining, face down

stitch edge above the zipper teeth

second exterior piece is on the bottom

Second lining piece, facedown

First lining piece, face up

STEP 4

stitch above the zipper teeth

Lining pieces, right sides together (leave bottom open)

zipper is inside this seam

STEP 5

Exterior pieces, right sides together

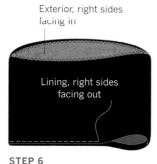

Exterior, right sides facing in

Lining, right sides facing out

STEP 6

SNIPPY TIP

Use pinking shears to trim the edges of the pouch, to help keep them from fraying.

6. **FINISH THE LINING.** Reach inside the pouch and unzip the zipper all the way (it will be upside down, but you can push the zipper slider to one side). Turn the lining right side out by folding it back over the exterior pieces. With the exterior inside the lining, turn under the bottom edge of the lining by about ¼" (with the folded edges tucked in toward each other). Stitch along the folded edges to close the bottom, making sure not to stitch the exterior pieces (it might help to pull them out through the zipper). Now turn the pouch right side out through the zipper opening and tuck the lining inside.

Get a Grip!

You can easily turn a zippered wristlet into a wristlet by adding a strap near the zipper. Here are some pointers:

strap is tucked inside

+ Measure out how long you'd like the strap to be and cut your fabric for the strap. We cut ours about 2" wide, which makes a ½"-wide strap when folded and stitched (*see page 42*).

+ Hint: If you cut the ends of the strap at an angle, it'll be easier to attach them to your pouch — plus, the pouch will hang more smoothly from your wrist.

✦ Add the strap at step 5 (*see page* 71), when you stitch the sides. Sandwich the strap between the two exterior fabric panels. You'll want them at the corner by the zipper, on the side where the zipper pull will be when the pouch is closed. Pin the strap in place and stitch the sides of the pouch, going through the ends of the strap.

POCKET CHANGE

For a cute little change purse, all you need are some 4" × 6" fabric scraps and a 6" zipper. Once you get the hang of making these, you can produce a unique gift in no time.

CHAPTER  *Totes*

THE TOTE BAG IS AS BASIC AS IT GETS. Long or short handles, pockets or no pockets, lined or unlined, you can make as many variations on the tote as you can think of. You'll never get tired of making them — or run out of uses for them! Try all three of the projects here, then branch out and make changes to suit your personal style and needs.

Tiny Tote

SKILL LEVEL
newbie

Totes are lovely in any size, but there's something so precious about a tiny one. This little cutie is great for those quick stops at the drugstore, and a good introduction to making custom bags. Develop your style by making a bunch. Play with different handle lengths and find fabric combinations that you love.

OUR FINISHED SIZE: 7" × 6", two 22½" straps

WHAT YOU'LL NEED

+ ¼ yard of fabric for the bag
+ ¼ yard of fabric for the handles
+ Sewing supplies (*see page* 18)

WHAT YOU'LL DO

+ Decide your size
+ Cut your fabric
+ Make and attach the straps
+ Stitch the sides and the top edge
+ Finish the straps

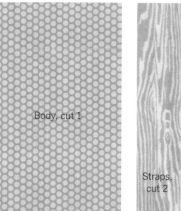

8"

3"

15"

Body, cut 1

Straps,
cut 2

23½"

Measure and Cut

1. **DECIDE YOUR SIZE.** We made our tiny tote pretty tiny — just big enough to hold keys, a cell phone, and some lip gloss. Follow our size, or modify it to hold your own "basics." For the body of the bag, decide on the width and add an inch for seam allowances; double the height and add 3" for the two folded top edges. For the handles, multiply the desired height of the bag by two, add enough inches for your desired strap length, include a few more inches for seams, and cut two strips of fabric of total length.

2. **CUT YOUR FABRIC.** Mark the pieces for the body and the straps on the wrong side of the fabrics. Cut one piece of fabric for the body of the bag and two strips of fabric of total length.

MIX IT UP!

You can make your entire tote from one fabric, or make the body from one fabric and the handle from another. Feel free to play with color, patterns, and textures — and thread color! If you want the colors to blend in, match your thread to the dominant color in your fabric. Or add some flair by letting the thread pop out a bit. Use a light or contrasting colored thread and see how fun your little tote can be!

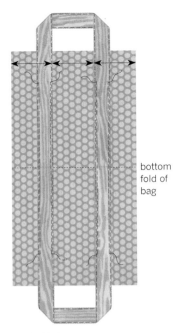

bag divided in thirds across the width

bottom fold of bag

STEP 4

Put It Together

3. **MAKE THE STRAPS.** Stitch the ends together to create one large loop. Fold and press the entire strip down the middle lengthwise, and then open and press under the sides by ½". Close middle fold and edgestitch along both sides (*see page* 42).

4. **ATTACH THE STRAPS.** Fold your bag fabric lengthwise in thirds, making two light creases for handle placement. With the handle seams at the halfway point on the bag (where the bag bottom will be), pin the handles along the creases. Stitch both sides of the strap to the bag, stopping 2" from the edges and backtacking.

5. **STITCH THE SIDES.** Fold the fabric panel in half with right sides together, lining up the top edges of the bag. Stitch the sides together and trim off excess seam allowance. Finish the raw edges as desired (*see page* 39).

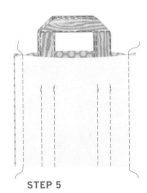

STEP 5

6. **STITCH THE TOP.** With the bag still wrong side out, press under the top raw edge ½". Press the edge under again 1" and edgestitch the bottom fold.

7. **FINISH THE STRAPS.** Turn bag right side out and finish edgestitching the straps to the top of the bag. Reinforce with a box stitch, if desired. (*See page* 43.)

boxstitch

STEP 7

Reversible Tote

Here's your chance to show your best side — twice! Use contrasting prints or complementary ones. Maybe you'd like a print on one side and a solid fabric on the other. Have fun and try as many combinations as you can think of.

OUR FINISHED SIZE: 14" × 15½", two 26" straps

WHAT YOU'LL NEED

+ 1 yard of fabric A
+ 1 yard of fabric B
+ Sewing supplies (*see page* 18)

WHAT YOU'LL DO

+ Decide your size
+ Cut your fabric
+ Make and attach the pockets
+ Stitch the sides
+ Assemble the bags
+ Make and attach the straps

Measure and Cut

1. **DECIDE YOUR SIZE.** Use our dimensions, or figure out what size bag you want to make and how long your straps will be. The tote we made is sized for magazines, but you can adapt yours to hold anything: a longer rectangle, a horizontal rectangle for your yarn, or a simple square tote for everyday. Be sure to play with the strap length before making your bag. You don't want your bag to hit you in an uncomfortable way or to drag on the ground. Once you find a length you like, keep the measurements listed somewhere so you can use them again. (*See page* 110.)

2. **CUT YOUR FABRIC.** On the wrong side of the fabrics, draw the outlines of the pieces and cut out identical pieces from both of the fabrics:

   + *two rectangles for the body*
   + *two strips for the handles*
   + *one rectangle for the pocket*

   ### SHORTCUT
   Draw the pieces on one of the fabrics, then lay it on top of the reverse fabric and cut the pieces from both fabrics at the same time.

CUT YOUR FABRIC

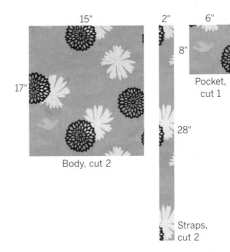

15"

17"

Body, cut 2

2"

8"

28"

Straps, cut 2

6"

Pocket, cut 1

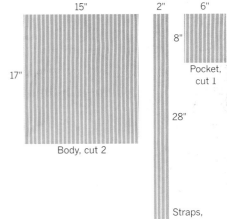

15"

17"

Body, cut 2

2"

8"

28"

Straps, cut 2

6"

Pocket, cut 1

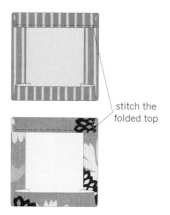

STEP 3

stitch the
folded top

STEP 4

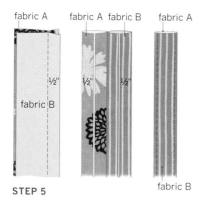

fabric A   fabric A fabric B   fabric A

½"   ½"   ½"

fabric B

fabric B

STEP 5

Put It Together

3. **MAKE AND ATTACH THE POCKETS.** On the sides and bottom of a pocket, press under ½". Press under the top edge ¼", then press under ½". Edgestitch the top fold in place as shown. (*See page* 43.) Pin the fabric A pocket onto a fabric B body panel, both with right sides facing out. Edgestitch around three sides of the pocket and backtack. Topstitch another line ¼" away from the first line and backtack. Repeat for the other pocket.

4. **STITCH THE BAG.** With right sides facing, pin matching body panels together for each fabric. Stitch the sides and bottom, using a ½" seam allowance. Trim excess seam allowance, and clip corners diagonally (*see page* 41). Leave the top unstitched for now. You will have two bags; turn one of them right side out, press the edges, and place the other bag inside it.

5. **MAKE THE STRAPS.** With right sides together, pin a fabric A strap to a fabric B strap. Stitch along one long side with a ½" seam allowance and press the seam open. Press under the raw edges on the sides ½". Fold the strap along the seam, match the folded edges, and edgestitch. Repeat with the second set of straps.

6. **ATTACH THE STRAPS.** While the bags are still nesting, press under 1" at top of each bag, and pin down. Matching a fabric A strap front with a fabric B panel, insert the strap ends between the top edges of both bags by about 1" and pin. Edgestitch the tops of the bags together. You might want to run an extra line of stitching to secure the straps.

straps are tucked between the two bags

STEP 6

HOKEY POKEY

Here's a tip: When tucking one bag into the other, use a chopstick to poke the corners out!

TAILOR-MADE TOTES

You can make your tote with short handles or long straps — it's up to you. For beginners, I'd suggest starting out at about 12" for short handles and about 30" for longer shoulder straps. Play with different lengths to find your favorites. Be sure to add 1" to 2" for tweaking and attaching the handles or straps.

Tool Tote

Imagine having everything you need right at your fingertips
— and then imagine that it's all portable! This tote can
accommodate any tools or supplies. You pick the size and
shape, and then let the bag do all the work.

OUR FINISHED SIZE: 10" × 15" × 5" deep, two 23" straps

WHAT YOU'LL NEED

+ ¾ yard of fabric for the bag
  (we used oilcloth)

+ ¾ yard of contrasting fabric
  for the handles, inside pocket,
  and pocket panel

+ Sewing supplies (*see page* 18)

WHAT YOU'LL DO

+ Decide your size

+ Cut your fabric

+ Make the pocket panel

+ Stitch the sides

+ Make the inside pocket

+ Stitch the top

+ Make and attach the straps
  and ties

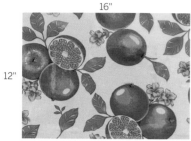

16"

12"

Front/back, cut 2

16"

6"

Bottom,
cut 1

12"

6"

Sides, cut 2

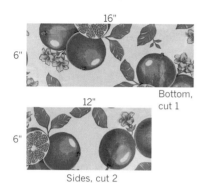

3"

Straps,
cut 2

4"

Inside
pocket,
cut 2

5"

9"

24"

1½"

16"

10"

cutoff

4½"

Ties, cut 2

Front
pocket,
cut 1

Measure and Cut

1. **DECIDE YOUR SIZE.** Figure out what size bag you want to make, how long your straps will be, and your desired pocket configuration. When planning your pockets, you can lay your tools out on the wrong side of the fabric and mark off the sizes you'll need. You'll need to make the height of the pockets a little shorter than your tools, so you can easily get them in and out. And be sure to add a little ease — this is especially important if the tools have some depth (*see page* 15).

2. **CUT YOUR FABRIC.** Measure and draw the bag pieces on the wrong side of the fabric and cut out the following:

   + *primary fabric: one front panel, one back panel, two side panels, and one bottom panel*
   + *contrasting fabric: and one front pocket panel, two inside pocket pieces, two straps, and two ties*

3. **MARK THE FRONT POCKET PANEL.** Decide what tools you'll want in the pocket panel and measure out slots for compartments on the right side of the fabric. Allow a little extra room for ease so the compartments won't be too tight.

Put It Together

4. **MAKE THE FRONT POCKET.** Press under the top diagonal edge ½" and edgestitch. Pin the pocket to the front of the bag, both with right sides facing out. Through both layers of fabric, stitch the pocket compartments along your markings, backtacking at the top for reinforcement. Leave the raw sides and bottom edges unstitched but pinned — or baste them in place ¼" from the edge, if you prefer.

Front of bag

STEP 4

5. **STITCH THE SIDES.** With right sides together, pin the short edges of the sides to the bottom piece. Stitch a ½" seam, stopping ½" from either end (as shown by the dots at right, 5a) and backtacking. With right sides together, pin the sides and bottom to the back bag panel and stitch, pivoting at the corners (5b). (The slits in the side seams will make it easier to turn the corners.) Repeat for the front of the bag.

Side | Bottom | Side

STEP 5a

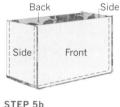

Back | Side

Side | Front

STEP 5b

6. **MAKE THE INSIDE POCKET.** On one inside pocket piece, press under the top edge ½", then repeat for another ½", and edgestitch. With right sides together, pin the side and bottom edges to the other pocket piece as shown. Stitch on three sides and backtack, clip the corners, and turn the pocket right side out. Press under the unstitched side seams.

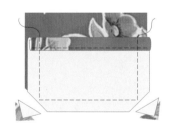

STEP 6

STEP 7

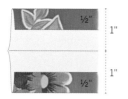

STEP 8

7. **STITCH THE TOP AND ATTACH THE POCKET.** Press under the top raw edge of the bag ½". Press under again 1". Center the pocket on the inside back hem of the bag and pin the pocket's unstitched edge under the folded hem. Edgestitch around the top edge of entire bag.

8. **MAKE AND ATTACH THE STRAPS.** Make two straps, following the instructions on page 42. On the outside of the bag, pin the ends of one strap on either side of the inside pocket. Pin the ends of the other strap at the same locations on the other side of the bag. Stitch the straps to the bag and reinforce with a box stitch. (*See page* 43.)

9. **MAKE AND ATTACH THE TIES.** Make the ties the same way you'd make a strap (*see page* 42), by pressing under the sides to meet in the center along the length. At the ends, open up the tie and press under ½". Refold the tie and press. Edgestitch the ties on all sides. Pin them at the top inside center of both the front and back of the bag. Stitch in place.

PROTECT YOUR STUFF

The bag shown on page 86 was made to hold knitting supplies, but you can make a tote to suit any craft or hobby: quilting, needlepoint, gardening, woodworking; you can even make totes for your household tools. For most tool bags, I suggest using a sturdy fabric such as canvas, denim, or even upholstery fabric. You don't want your pockets to slump over with the weight of your pruning shears. And you don't want your knitting needles to poke through that lovely linen you've been waiting to use on something special. If you will be toting softer, lighter tools, you can go with something less durable.

We used a heavyweight canvas for the Tool Holster that carries pruning shears (*see page* 139).

FABRIC IDEA

Mexican oilcloth is a specialty fabric that is affordable, durable, water-resistant, and easy to clean. It comes in a wide array of vibrant and cheerful prints, and is sold in fabric and craft stores. Note that the colors may fade, and when using this heavier weight fabric you'll need to use strong thread and extra stitching reinforcement.

CHAPTER  *Drawstring Sacks*

ANOTHER SIMPLE BUT INCREDIBLY USEFUL BAG STYLE
is the drawstring sack. Customize the sizes and drawstrings
to make a wrist bag, a bag to hold notions, a lingerie storage
bag, and more! For kids, you can modify the drawstring
backpack size to fit a smaller frame. You can also make little
travel bags to help organize your packing. Make a bunch and
see how many uses they have!

Ditty Bag

Versatile, fun, and easy to make, the ditty bag has endless possibilities. Make them in almost any size and from any fabric. We used fabric for our drawstring, but you can use ribbon, cord, shoestrings, or twill tape.

OUR FINISHED SIZE: 7½" × 9½"

WHAT YOU'LL NEED

+ ¼ yard of fabric for the bag

+ 20" of fabric cord or ribbon for the drawstring

+ Sewing supplies (*see page* 18)

WHAT YOU'LL DO

+ Decide your size

+ Cut your fabric

+ Stitch the sides

+ Make the casing

+ Insert the drawstring

CUT YOUR FABRIC

8½"

11"

Body, cut 2

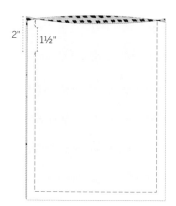

2"   1½"

STEP 3

Measure and Cut

1. **DECIDE YOUR SIZE.** A simple drawstring bag can serve many purposes: holding laundry, wine, shoes, marbles (sure, marbles!), or even your lunch. You can use fancier, heavier weight fabrics to make a sweet handbag.

2. **CUT YOUR FABRIC.** Fold the fabric in half lengthwise, right sides together. On the wrong side of the fabric, draw a rectangle that is the desired size of your bag. Add 1" to the width for side seams, and 2½" to the length for the casing and bottom seam. Cut two pieces. If making a fabric drawstring, cut a strip 3" wide and the desired length (*see below*).

> **HOW MUCH STRING?**
>
> Whether you're making a fabric drawstring (*see page 42*) or using ribbon or a cord, you'll need to figure out the length. Simply double the width of the bag and add a few extra inches for finishing and knotting the ends.

Put It Together

3. **STITCH THE SIDES.** With right sides together, stitch down one side, across the bottom, and up the other side, stopping 2" from the top. Backtack and cut the thread. Leaving a 1½" gap, stitch the last ½" to the top edge, backtacking on both ends. Press the seam open and stitch about 2" down the seam

allowances on either side of the opening. Clip the bottom corners and trim the seam allowance.

4. **MAKE THE CASING.** Press under ½" of the top raw edge, then press under another 1½". Edgestitch along the bottom of fold. (*See page* 44).

5. **INSERT THE DRAWSTRING.** Using a safety pin, thread the ribbon or cord through hole and around to the other side. (*See page* 45). Knot the ends.

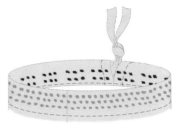

STEP 5

DOO-WAH DITTY

The drawstring bag is ideal for gift giving. Make a bag to suit someone's special needs, or use it as the gift wrap! Some suggestions:

✦ Who wants to haul around a big, ugly laundry bag? A homemade drawstring laundry sack makes a wonderful gift for students and campers.

✦ Going to a dinner party? Why not wrap that bottle of wine in a snazzy drawstring bag that adds a personal touch. For our wine-bottle gift bag, we made the drawstring casing a little lower than on the other bags (about 1½" from the the top edge) so it could be pulled around the neck of the bottle for a prettier presentation.

Backpack

SKILL LEVEL
pro

Cute and practical, this drawstring backpack can be made to fit your body, the contents of the pack, or both. Try different sizes for different needs, such as gym gear, sleepover supplies, or a school bag. You can also use rope or ribbon for the straps. Just cut them to the desired length and thread them through the casing as described, instead of using fabric straps.

OUR FINISHED SIZE: 13" × 18", two 60" straps

WHAT YOU'LL NEED

+ ¾ yard of fabric for the bag
+ ½ yard of fabric for straps and pockets (could be matching or different)
+ Sewing supplies (*see page* 18)

WHAT YOU'LL DO

+ Decide your size
+ Cut your fabric
+ Make and attach the pocket
+ Stitch the sides
+ Make a casing
+ Make and attach the straps

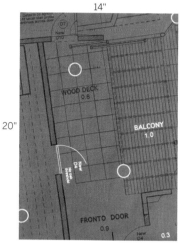

14"

20"

Front/back, cut 2

6"

2"

7½"

31"

Pocket, cut 1

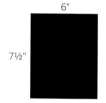

Straps, cut 4

Measure and Cut

1. **DECIDE YOUR SIZE.** You can build a backpack to carry your groceries, take your stuff to the gym, or use as a funky everyday purse. Bring out your gear or gadgets and lay them out. How much space do you need? We added one pocket to our pack, but you could easily tack on a few if you want more of them. Try a few variations.

2. **CUT YOUR FABRIC.** Draw the pieces on the wrong side of the fabric and cut out the following:
   + *two backpack panels*
   + *two straps (suggested finished length 60"). If you are making a smaller or larger pack, here's how you figure strap length: They need to be at least the width plus the height of your pack, multiplied by two. Then add a few inches for finishing and knotting the ends.*
   + *one pocket*

Put It Together

3. **MAKE AND ATTACH THE POCKET.** Make a pocket as described on page 43. With both pieces right side up, pin the pocket onto the front backpack panel. (Ours is centered about 4" from the bottom.) Edgestitch around three sides of the pocket, backtacking at ends. Topstitch another line ¼" away from the first line and backtack.

4. **STITCH THE SIDES.** With right sides together, pin the backpack along the sides and bottom edge. Measure and mark 1½" and 2½" down from the top of each side. This will become the top slot for the straps. Along the bottom edge, measure and mark ½" (which will be the seam allowance) and another ½" in from the sides. This will be the bottom slot for the straps. Stitch the sides and the bottom between the marks as shown, backtacking at the start and end of all stitching.

2½"   1½"

½"

STEP 4

5. **MAKE A CASING.** Press open the backpack side seams and stitch on either side of the opening (*see pages 44–45*.) Press under the top raw edges ½", then repeat for another 1". Edgestitch along the bottom fold. Turn the backpack right side out.

6. **MAKE AND ATTACH THE STRAPS.** Stitch the short end of two 31" strips together to make one long 60" strap. Repeat with the remaining two strap pieces. Make two straps as described on page 42. The finished straps will be ½" wide. Thread each strap through the top casing, one through the front and one through the back. On the bottom of the pack, slide two ends into each of the ½" slots at the side corners, knot them, and pin them into place. Turn the pack wrong side out and stitch the corner openings closed with the knots inside, backtacking to reinforce. Trim the seams, turn the bag right side out, and press.

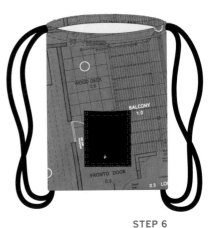

STEP 6

Sling Sack

Originally designed to hold clothespins, the Sling Sack can be a great help when hanging laundry out in the fresh spring air. It is also easily tailored for other uses, this bag is ideal for crafters, painters, or makeup artists — anyone who needs to cart around special supplies in an expandable sack.

OUR FINISHED SIZE: 12" × 13", 30" strap

WHAT YOU'LL NEED

+ ¾ yard of fabric for the bag and strap
+ ½ yard of contrasting fabric for pockets and the top panel
+ 28" of fabric, cord, or ribbon for the drawstring (optional)
+ Sewing supplies (*see page* 18)

WHAT YOU'LL DO

+ Decide your size
+ Cut your fabric
+ Make the pocket panel
+ Stitch the bag
+ Make and attach the strap
+ Make the casing and the drawstring (optional)

CUT YOUR FABRIC

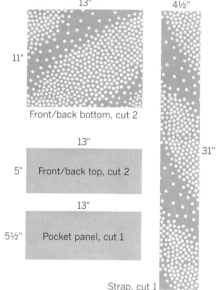

13"

11"

Front/back bottom, cut 2

13"

5" Front/back top, cut 2

13"

5½" Pocket panel, cut 1

4½"

31"

Strap, cut 1

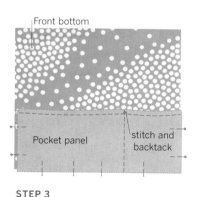

Front bottom

Pocket panel | stitch and backtack

STEP 3

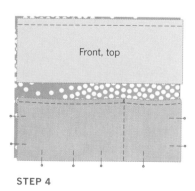

Front, top

STEP 4

Measure and Cut

1. **DECIDE YOUR SIZE.** The main compartment is a nice pouch for holding stuff like yarn or clothespins. The front pockets allow easy access to essentials. Figure out what size bag you want to make and how long your straps will be.

2. **CUT YOUR FABRIC.** Draw the pieces on the wrong side of the fabric and cut out the following:
   * *from primary fabric: two bottom pieces and one strap (optional: cut a 1½" × 32" strip for a drawstring)*
   * *from contrasting fabric: two top panels and one pocket panel*

3. **MAKE THE POCKET PANEL.** Press under the top of the pocket panel ¼", then repeat for another ¼". Edgestitch the bottom fold. With the right sides facing out, pin the pocket to a bottom piece. Stitch the sides and compartments as desired, backtacking at the top edge of the pocket.

4. **ATTACH THE TOP AND BOTTOM PIECES.** With right sides together, stitch each top panel to a bottom piece. Flip up each top section to extend the bag fully, and press.

5. **MAKE THE STRAP.** Fold the strap fabric in half lengthwise and press. Stitch the long side. (*See page* 42.) Trim the excess seam allowance and

turn the strap right side out. Press. If you like, edgestitch on both sides of the strap, but since ours is a lightweight bag, we skipped that step.

6. **ATTACH THE STRAP.** Cut the ends of the strap at an angle and pin them to the sides of the right side of the back of the bag (at the top of the bottom piece) as shown. Lay the front side of the bag on top; the strap ends will be sandwiched between the front and back pieces. Stitch the sides and bottom of the bag, stopping 2½" short at the top of one side and backtacking. Leave a 1" opening and then stitch to the top edge, backtacking on both ends. Clip the corners and trim the seam allowance.

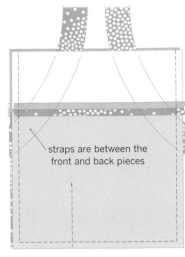

straps are between the front and back pieces

STEP 6

> **DRAWSTRING VARIATION**
>
> If you want the drawstring to extend on both sides, stop short by 2½" and leave a 1" opening on both sides when stitching in step 6. When you make the casing, you'll have an opening on both sides of the bag.

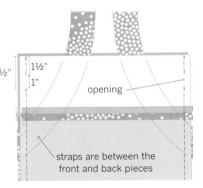

2½" 1½" 1" opening

straps are between the front and back pieces

STEP 6 (variation)

7. **MAKE THE CASING.** Press under the top edge of the bag ½", and then repeat for under another 1". Edgestitch along the first fold. (*See page* 44.) Use ribbon or cording for a drawstring, or make your own from fabric. (*See page* 45). Use a safety pin to thread the drawstring through the opening on one side. Tie the two ends together with a knot.

CHAPTER  *Messenger Bags*

FOR SCHOOL, WORK, CITY LIVING, OR TRAVEL —

the messenger bag can't be beat. It's an easy shape to work

with, and can be lined or unlined. You can customize the

pocket configurations in a million different ways!

Personal Purse

This simple purse can be designed to suit your individual needs and taste. Customize it to fit your daily essentials. This one has pockets for gadgets like a phone or MP3 player. You can add a zipper to the main compartment or a flap on top — or both, as we've done here.

OUR FINISHED SIZE: 8" × 10", 52" strap

WHAT YOU'LL NEED

+ ½–³⁄₈ yard of fabric for the bag and strap
+ ½ yard of contrasting fabric for the flap and pockets
+ 1 matching zipper (optional) at least as wide as the purse (we used an 11" zipper)
+ Sewing supplies (*see page* 18)

WHAT YOU'LL DO

+ Decide your size
+ Cut your fabric
+ Make the pocket panel
+ Make and attach the flap
+ Attach the zipper (optional)
+ Make and attach the strap
+ Stitch and turn your bag

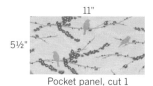

5½" 11"

Pocket panel, cut 1

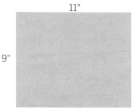

8" 11"

Flap, cut 2

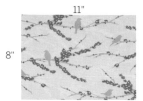

9" 11"

Body, cut 2

3"

27"

Strap, cut 2

Measure and Cut

1. **DECIDE YOUR SIZE.** You can base the size of your purse on the pockets, the main compartment, or both. If you have a lot of little things to keep track of, I suggest starting with your pockets. Pick the most important items and lay them on top of your pocket fabric. Mark the pocket lines carefully and be sure to add a little ease (make the pockets a little wider than your gadgets, which is especially important if your gadget is not flat). If you are planning to carry something a bit bigger, like a notebook, then use it to determine the size of the bag first. You can add pockets to that and customize them as needed.

MAKE IT TO FIT

If you plan to carry your bag on your shoulder, measure from the top of your shoulder to your hip. Double that number to determine the length of your strap. If you plan to carry your bag with the strap across your chest, add another 6" to 8". It's always best to add yet another couple of inches for tweaking and attaching the strap. It's much easier to cut a strap shorter than to start over to make a longer one!

2. **CUT YOUR FABRIC.** Measure and draw the bag pieces on the wrong side of the fabric and cut out the following:

- *primary fabric: two body pieces and two strap pieces*
- *contrasting fabric: one pocket panel and two flap pieces*

3. **MARK THE POCKET PANEL.** Decide what you'll want to carry in the pocket panel and measure out slots for compartments on the right side of the fabric.

Put It Together

4. **MAKE THE POCKETS.** Press under the top of the pocket ¼", then press under another ¼". Pin and edgestitch the bottom fold. With right sides facing up, pin the pocket to the front panel, lining up the raw edges. Stitch the compartments as desired and backtack at the top edges.

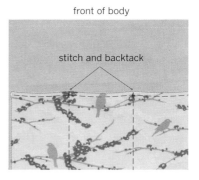

front of body

stitch and backtack

STEP 4

5. **MAKE AND ATTACH THE FLAP (OPTIONAL).** Pin the two flap pieces with right sides together and stitch the sides and bottom. Clip the corners and trim the seam allowances. Turn the flap right side out, press, and with right sides together, baste the flap to the back bag panel. (Make sure you are basting to the *back* of the purse, not the side with the pocket panel.)

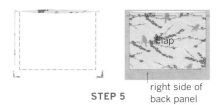

Flap

STEP 5

right side of back panel

6. **ATTACH THE ZIPPER (OPTIONAL).** It helps to take the zipper installation one step at a time. (*See the next page.*)

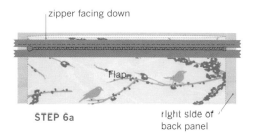

zipper facing down

STEP 6a

right side of
back panel

Flap

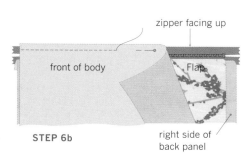

zipper facing up

front of body

Flap

STEP 6b

right side of
back panel

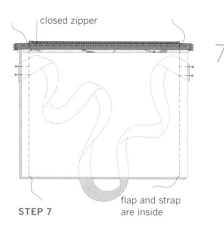

closed zipper

STEP 7

flap and strap
are inside

a. Place the closed zipper facedown on the edge you just basted in step 5. Line up the edge of the zipper with the raw edge of the fabric, pin, and stitch. When you come to the zipper pull, stop stitching. Leave your needle in the fabric while you slide the zipper pull out of the way, and then continue stitching.

b. To attach the front panel, turn the zipper up, away from the body of the bag and press the bag away from the zipper. Lay the front of the bag facedown on top of the zipper and align the top edges (this should not be the edge with the pocket panel). Pin and then stitch the top edge, as you did with the other side of the zipper. After stitching, flip the top layer away from the zipper to get a feel for how the bag is coming together. You should be able to see the zipper teeth at the top and the attached flap. The sides and bottom of the bag are not yet stitched.

7. **MAKE AND ATTACH THE STRAP.** Stitch the short ends of two 27" strips together to make one long 53" strap. Make a strap as instructed on page 42, and cut the ends of the strap at an angle. Pin the ends to each side edge of the front panel's right side, near the zipper. Lay the back of the bag on top with right sides together and the zipper closed. The strap and the flap should be tucked inside. Pin

in place. Stitch up the sides of the bag and straps, going through the zipper, and backtack.

8. **STITCH AND TURN THE BAG.** Open the zipper. Stitch the bottom of the bag and up both sides an inch or so for reinforcement, backtacking at the ends. Clip the corners and trim the seam allowance. You might also want to add a zigzag stitch to the seam edges to prevent fraying. Turn the bag right side out through the zipper opening, and press.

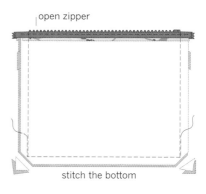

STEP 8

Options Galore

UNZIPPED. If you want to make the personal purse without a zipper, just leave out step 6 above. Instead, turn under the top edge of the bag ¼" and press, then turn under another ¼", press and stitch. Or, you daredevils might want to add a lining (*see DJ Bag for lining instructions*).

UNFLAPPABLE. If you'd like to keep the zipper but lose the flap, simply skip step 5. You'll have a zip-top purse with even easier access to the front pockets.

MAXIMUM SECURITY. Secure your flap by adding a closure such as Velcro, some snaps, or a button and a buttonhole.

CUSTOMIZE. Changing the shape and pocket layout can turn a simple purse into a perfect travel bag (*at right*). A zippered side pouch adds an extra safety slot. It's all about the details — your details!

DJ Bag

A simple messenger bag can hold just about anything. The traditional shape of a DJ bag is a square (to hold record albums), but you can experiment to get the best shape for your needs. You can make a DJ bag to carry your books, art supplies, or magazines, or use it as a nontraditional handbag.

OUR FINISHED SIZE: 15" × 15" × 3" deep, 43" strap

WHAT YOU'LL NEED

+ 1 yard of fabric for bag front, back, and flap (we used mid-weight canvas)

+ ½ yard of fabric for the straps and sides of bag (we used denim)

+ ¾ yard of fabric for the lining (optional)

+ Sewing supplies (*see page 18*)

WHAT YOU'LL DO

+ Decide your size

+ Cut your fabric

+ Stitch the bag

+ Make and attach the flap

+ Make and attach strap

+ Line the bag (optional)

CUT YOUR FABRIC

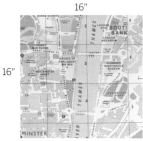

16"

16"

Front/back, cut 2

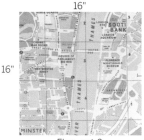

16"

16"

Flap, cut 2

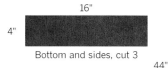

16"

4"

Bottom and sides, cut 3

16"

16"

Lining front/back, cut 2

16"

4"

Lining bottom and sides, cut 3

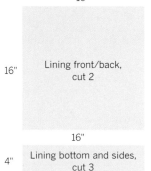

6"

44"

Strap, cut 1

Measure and Cut

1. **DECIDE YOUR SIZE.** Figure out what you'll carry in your DJ bag and base your size on those items. Feel free to make the bag deeper than the 3" we made ours if you need the space. Be sure to choose fabrics that will hold your desired contents well. If you'll use it like a purse, then cotton is A-OK. But if you plan to really stuff it or to carry bulky, heavy things like books and such, I suggest a heavier weight fabric like canvas or denim — or both, like we used here.

> **STRAP LENGTH**
>
> To get a good measurement for your strap: take your measuring tape or some string and measure from your hip across your chest to your shoulder and back again to your hip.

2. **CUT YOUR FABRIC.** Draw the pieces on the wrong side of the fabric and cut out the following (the front/back, flap, and lining pieces are all the same size, but we've separated them out since you might want to make them from different fabrics):

   + *featured fabric: one front, one back, and two flap pieces*
   + *denim: two sides, one bottom, and one strap*
   + *lining (optional): one front, one back, two sides, and one bottom*

Put It Together

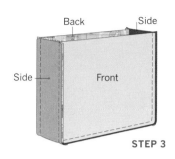

3. **STITCH THE BODY OF BAG.** With right sides together, stitch the sides and bottom strips into one long piece, stopping ½" from each end of the seam and backtacking. Press the seams toward the center. With right sides together, pin the front panel to the strip. Stitch the seam, pivoting at the corners, and press. Attach the back panel in the same way.

STEP 3

4. **MAKE AND ATTACH THE FLAP.** With right sides facing, stitch the two flap pieces together on three sides. Trim the seam allowance, clip the corners, turn the flap right side out, and press. Pin the flap to the back of the bag as shown and stitch.

stitch the flap

turn the flap and stitch to back of bag

5. **MAKE AND ATTACH THE STRAP.** Fold the strap in half lengthwise, right sides facing, and stitch the entire length. Turn it right side out and press. (*See page 42.*) With right sides together, pin the ends of the straps to the sides of the bag, stitch, and backtack.

STEP 4

6. **LINE THE BAG (OPTIONAL).** With right sides together, stitch the lining pieces together in the same way as the body of the bag (step 3), leaving an opening (about 4" or 5" long) on one side of a bottom seam. Press the seam allowances open. Turn the bag right side out and place it (straps, flap, and all) into the lining, which should be wrong side out (*see the next page*). With right sides together, pin the bag into the lining (the flap

flap is in back

STEP 5

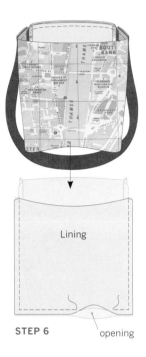

STEP 6   opening

and straps will be between the two layers). Stitch the top edges together, and trim the excess. Turn the bag right side out by pulling it through the opening in the lining. Turn under the edges of the liner opening, pin, and edgestitch.

TO LINE OR NOT TO LINE

If you are not lining your bag, it's a good idea to use a zigzag stitch on your raw edges. This will reinforce your bag so the fabric won't fray and the bag won't fall apart down the road. Another idea is to use bias tape to bind the edges. (*See page* 46.)

HEAVY DUTY

The Messenger style is a great option for a laptop bag. But keep in mind that a laptop needs serious cushioning and secure sewing. If you want to beef up your bag, here are a few options that'll do the trick:

+ **FABRIC.** Choose sturdy fabrics like canvas, cotton duck, denim, or anything labeled "upholstery" or "home decor" weight. You can also use heavier weight thread and make sure your stitching is secure.

+ **INTERFACING.** If you're looking for more structure, you can attach interfacing to most fabrics. You just apply the interfacing to the wrong side of the fabric at the beginning of the project and then continue as you normally would.

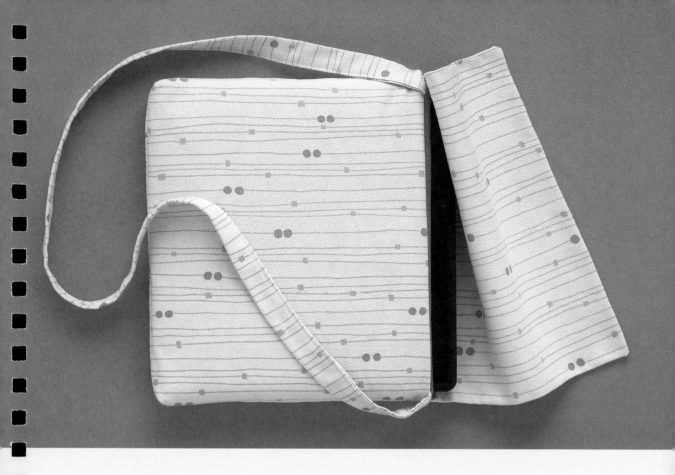

- ✦ **PADDING.** To protect your goodies inside, you can use a soft, plush lining like fleece, flannel, or corduroy. If you need extra cushioning, you should probably add some foam or batting. To add the foam or batting, you'll need to leave an opening and insert the padding just before stitching up the panels. (*See the* Artist's Roll *on page* 133.)

- ✦ **LINING.** If you are lining your bag, like this one, you'll probably want to leave a wider opening in the lining to pull the bag through, depending on the combined thickness of your beefy extras: the fabric, batting, and interfacing.

Ask your local shop for advice when choosing padding and interfacing. There are plenty of options and a little help will go a long way. Whatever you choose, it should have manufacturer's directions to help you out, too.

City Satchel

This signature bag is used by couriers all over the world. Make it rugged for the road warrior in you, classic enough for the office, or hip enough for hitting the streets. Choose your fabrics, size, and pocket configuration to suit your personal style and needs.

OUR FINISHED SIZE: 12" × 17" × 4" deep, 43" strap

WHAT YOU'LL NEED

+ 1¼ yards of fabric for the bag and strap

+ ¾ yard of fabric for the flap and pockets

+ ½ yard of fabric for the lining (optional)

+ Sewing supplies (*see page* 18)

WHAT YOU'LL DO

+ Decide your size

+ Cut your fabric

+ Make and attach the pockets

+ Stitch the bag

+ Make and attach the strap

+ Make and attach the flap

+ Line the bag (optional)

CUT YOUR FABRIC

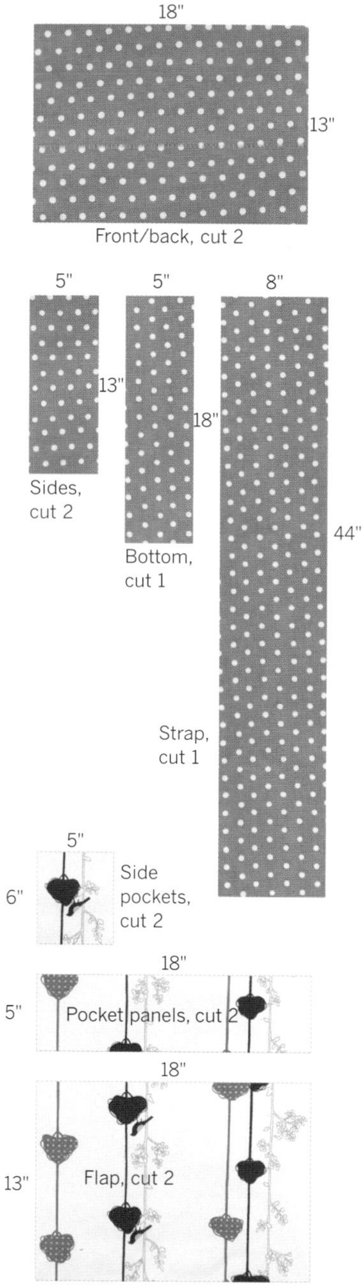

18"

Front/back, cut 2

13"

5" 5" 8"

Sides, cut 2

13"

18"

Bottom, cut 1

44"

Strap, cut 1

5"

6"

Side pockets, cut 2

18"

5" Pocket panels, cut 2

18"

13" Flap, cut 2

Measure and Cut

1. **DECIDE YOUR SIZE.** You might want this bag for work or school, or maybe for the gym. Whatever you decide, you can tailor this bag to suit your needs perfectly. Just put a little planning into it before you get started. Figure out what size bag you want to make and how long your strap will be.

> **REMINDER**
>
> To get a good measurement for your strap: take measuring tape or some string and measure from your hip across your chest to your shoulder, and back again to your hip.

2. **CUT YOUR FABRIC.** Draw the pieces on the wrong side of the fabric and cut out the following:

   + *primary fabric: one front, one back, two sides, one bottom, and one strap*
   + *contrasting fabric: two flap pieces, one front and one back pocket panel, and two side pockets*

Put It Together

3. **MAKE THE SIDE POCKETS.** Press under the top of the side pocket ¼", then again another ¼". Edgestitch along the bottom fold. Repeat with other pocket. Pin the pockets to the side panels, right sides facing out. (The pockets should be the same width

as the side panels, so stitching the side seams will hold the pockets in place.)

GOT A ROCKET IN YOUR POCKET?

This bag has enough pockets to fit anything you want them to, so think about what you'd like to bring along in your satchel. Your phone and MP3 player? How about your checkbook and your shades? A notebook and some pens? I always need a designated pocket for my keys, some gum, and my favorite tape measure. Have fun and plan your pockets to fit your stuff, your way.

CORNER POCKET

A couple of things to consider when you are choosing the size and placement of your pockets:

✦ Pocket height should be played with until you are sure you like where it is. If your pocket is too high up on the bag or too short, items may stick out of it. If the pockets are too low or too deep, you may have trouble getting to your stuff.

✦ If the pockets are not strong enough at the top, the fabric will sag and your goodies will fall out. It's a good idea to use bias tape to bind the top of your pockets (see page 46), or to double-stitch them for reinforcement.

Front of bag

Back of bag

STEP 4

4. **MAKE THE POCKET PANELS.** Press the top of the front pocket panel under ¼" and again ¼". Edgestitch along the bottom fold. Also, press under the bottom edge ¼" and edgestitch. Position and pin the pocket to the front bag panel. (We lined up the bottom of this panel with the top of the side pockets, but place it wherever you like.) Stitch along the bottom. Using chalk or pencil, mark dividing lines for pockets, based on your needs. Stitch along the dividing lines, backtacking at both ends. Do the same for the back, but if you are placing this pocket at the bottom seam, like ours, there is no need to turn under the bottom edge; it will be stitched into the seams of the bag.

5. **STITCH THE BAG.** With right sides together, pin the sides and bottom panels into one long strip. Make sure the side panels are placed with the pocket tops facing the right way. Stitch the seams, starting and ending ½" from the edges (as shown with dots) and backtacking. Press seams open. With right sides together, pin the sides and bottom to the front panel. Stitch with sides on top, pivoting at the corners. Attach the sides and bottom to the back panel of the bag in the same way. Press seams open.

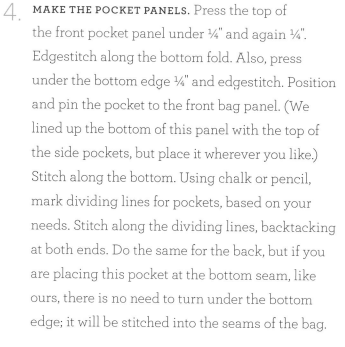

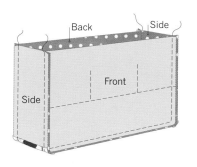

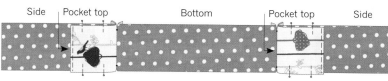

STEP 5

6. **MAKE AND ATTACH THE STRAP.** With right sides together, fold the strap in half lengthwise and stitch the entire length. Trim the seam allowance, turn the strap right side out, and press. (*See page* 42.) Edgestitch if you like. With right sides together, pin the ends of the strap to the top edges of the side panels, and stitch.

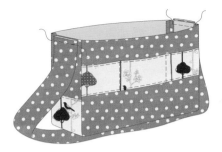

STEP 6

7. **MAKE AND ATTACH THE FLAP.** With right sides together, pin and stitch the flap pieces together along the sides and the bottom. Trim the seam allowance, clip the corners, turn the flap right side out, and press. Line up the raw edges of the flap to the back panel and pin. Stitch the flap to the back panel. Trim excess seam allowance and press.

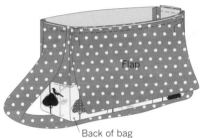

Flap

Back of bag

STEP 7

MAKE IT YOUR WAY

If you are not lining your bag, press the top edge under ½" and edgestitch. Another option is to bind the raw edges together before pressing them under (*see page* 46.).

8. **LINE THE BAG (OPTIONAL).** See the DJ Bag for lining instructions. The same steps apply here. For this bag, we chose a chocolate-brown lining.

OPTIONAL LINING

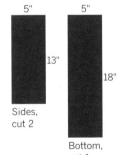

5"

5"

13"

18"

Sides, cut 2

Bottom, cut 1

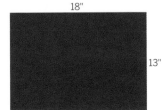

18"

13"

Front/back, cut 2

CHAPTER **7** *Organizers*

ORGANIZERS ARE GREAT FUN TO MAKE because of the endless variations you can come up with. Caddies, roll-ups, and aprons can be used in the kitchen, craft room, garden, bedroom, home office — you name it. These projects can easily be modified to fit your own supplies, tools, and body.

Tool Apron

We made this apron to hold quilting supplies, but you can customize yours for any craft, hobby, or project. Be sure to choose your fabrics and pockets to suit the job. For gardening tools, you'll want canvas or maybe oilcloth. For crochet supplies, you'll want a variety of pocket sizes for slim hooks and skeins of yarn.

OUR FINISHED SIZE: 8" × 16" with a 66" belt

WHAT YOU'LL NEED

- ✦ ⅜ yard of fabric for the apron body
- ✦ ½ yard of contrasting fabric for pockets and belt.
- ✦ Sewing supplies (*see page* 18)

WHAT YOU'LL DO

- ✦ Decide your size
- ✦ Cut your fabric
- ✦ Make the pocket
- ✦ Assemble the apron
- ✦ Make and attach the belt

Front and
back, cut 2   17"

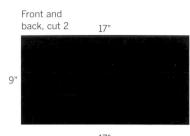

9"

17"

6"

Pocket panel,
cut 1

4"

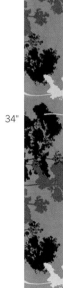

34"

Belt, cut 2

Measure and Cut

1. **DECIDE YOUR SIZE.** For a good fit, base the size on your favorite kitchen apron, or measure your torso from hip to hip and add a couple of inches for seam allowance. For the height, measure from your waist (or hip, if you like to wear it low) down to anywhere you like. It's your tool apron, so make it as long — or short — as you need it to be.

EASE INTO IT

Figure out how big your pockets need to be before you finalize the size of the apron. Lay your tools out on your fabric and measure them. Be sure to allow for some ease (a little bit of extra room to get your objects in and out of the pockets). Keep your tools handy while you're sewing and test along the way to make sure you've got a good fit.

2. **CUT YOUR FABRIC.** Based on your measurements, cut:
   + *primary fabric: one front and one back piece*
   + *contrasting fabric: one pocket panel and two belt pieces (We cut ours 4" wide for a finished width of 1½". For the total length of the belt, we measured around the waist, and then added 16" for tying the ends.)*

Put It Together

3. **MAKE THE POCKET.** Press under the top edge of pocket panel ¼", then repeat for another ½". Edgestitch along the bottom fold. With right sides facing up, pin the pocket panel to front apron panel. Based on your measurements, stitch dividers for your pockets, backtacking at the top of the pocket panel. There's no need to stitch the sides or bottom, as that will happen in the next step.

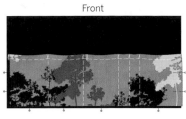

STEP 3

4. **ASSEMBLE THE APRON.** Lay the back apron piece on top of the front piece, right sides together. Stitch the sides and bottom, leaving the top of the apron open. Clip the corners, trim the seam allowance, turn the apron right side out, and press. Fold under the top edge ½" to the inside, press, and topstitch.

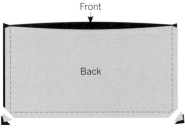

STEP 4

5. **MAKE AND ATTACH THE BELT.** With right sides facing, stitch the two belt pieces together to make one long strip. Press under the edges ½" on all sides, fold it in half lengthwise, and topstitch. (See page 42.) Center the belt on top of the apron, aligning the top edges of the belt and apron. Pin the belt in place and topstitch it to the apron along the length (following the stitching on both sides of the belt), backtacking at the ends.

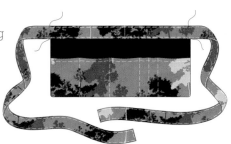

STEP 5

Artist's Roll

We made our roll for paintbrushes, but change the pocket configuration and you can store all kinds of tools, like knitting needles, carving tools, or pencils. You can add batting for extra protection, and combine fabrics to create your own look and feel. Pack up your tools your own way!

OUR FINISHED SIZE: 16" × 19" (open), 15½" × 6" (rolled)

WHAT YOU'LL NEED

+ ½ yard fabric for exterior of roll
+ ½ yard fabric for interior of roll
+ ½–¾ yard fabric for pockets
+ 1 yard bias tape (optional)
+ ¾ yard ⅜"-wide ribbon for the closure
+ ½ yard batting (optional)
+ Sewing supplies (*see page* 18)

WHAT YOU'LL DO

+ Decide your size
+ Cut your fabric and ribbon
+ Make and attach the pocket panels
+ Attach the ribbon
+ Stitch the sides
+ Add batting (optional)
+ Stitch the compartments

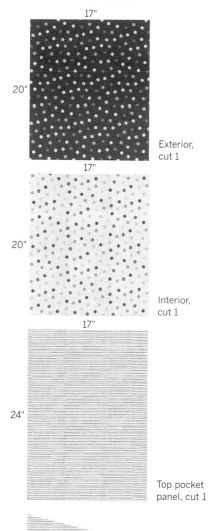

CUT YOUR FABRIC

17"

20"

Exterior,
cut 1

17"

20"

Interior,
cut 1

17"

24"

Top pocket
panel, cut 1

9"

17"

5"

17"

9"

5"

17"

Lower pocket panel, cut 2
facing in opposite directions

Measure and Cut

1. **DECIDE YOUR SIZE.** You can go by our dimensions, or make a roll to fit your own needs. (You might want to make ours first, to get a feel for how it goes together.)

CUSTOMIZING THE ROLL

To figure out your own size, lay out your tools on the right side of the exterior fabric to see how big your roll should be and how many pockets you'll need. Be sure to allow for ease (room to get your tools in and out of the pockets). When you're sure of the size of the roll, draw the shape and mark the divider lines for the pockets on the right side with dressmaker's chalk, disappearing marker, or pins. (The roll and both pockets will be stitched at the same time, so you only need to mark one piece.) Cut the other pieces to match your prototype. Keep your tools nearby in case you need to tweak the pocket widths before stitching them.

2. **CUT YOUR FABRIC.** Draw the pieces on the wrong side of the fabric and cut out the following (any of these pieces can be cut from the same fabric or contrasting fabric).

   ✦ *one interior and one exterior piece*
   ✦ *one rectangular pocket panel*
   ✦ *two diagonal pocket panel pieces*

Put It Together

3. **MAKE THE POCKET PANELS.** With right sides together, stitch the lower pocket pieces along the diagonal edge. Press the seam open, then put wrong sides together and press. If adding bias tape, enclose the diagonal edge (with the narrow edge of the tape on top) and edgestitch. For the top pocket, fold the rectangular pocket in half (to make it 12" × 17"), press, and add bias tape to one long side in the same way.

STEP 3

4. **ATTACH THE POCKET PANELS.** On the right side of the interior piece, pin the two pocket panels and baste around the outer edges as shown.

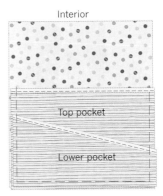

Interior

Top pocket

Lower pocket

STEP 4

5. **ATTACH THE RIBBON.** On the right side of the exterior piece, position the ribbon in the center as shown, in the direction the fabric will be rolled. Stitch the ribbon in place, backtacking to make sure it's secure. For a decorative touch, clip a little "V" in the ends of the ribbon.

Exterior

STEP 5

HOW MUCH RIBBON?

Figure the length of your ribbon ties by multiplying the width of the folded case by 2, and then adding enough extra to tie a bow. Cut more than you think you'll need, and trim it to fit. If the roll is heavy when filled, you may want to wrap the ribbon around it twice.

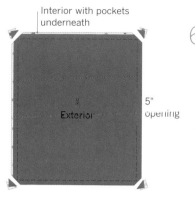

Interior with pockets underneath

Exterior

5" opening

STEP 6

6. **STITCH THE SIDES.** Lay the exterior piece on top of the interior piece with right sides together (the pockets and the ribbon will be facing each other). Tuck the ends of the ribbon between the layers. Stitch the pieces together on all four sides, leaving a 5" opening along one side. Trim the seam allowance to within ¼" of seam, clip the corners, and turn the roll right side out through the opening. Press.

STEP 7

7. **ADD BATTING (OPTIONAL).** If you want to add batting, now is the time to do it. Cut the batting to fit the size of the stitched roll, making it slightly smaller to fit within the seams. Roll the batting into a tube shape and insert it into the opening. Flatten it out by reaching in and smoothing it out to the corners. Trim to fit if necessary.

> **A BIT OF PADDING**
>
> The batting is a nice touch because it gives your roll more structure and offers your tools extra protection. This is a must if you have fancy or delicate needles!

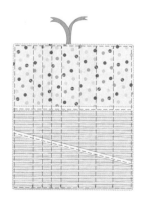

STEP 8

8. **STITCH THE COMPARTMENTS.** Tuck in and pin the seam allowances at the 5" opening, and then topstitch around all four sides. If you drew customized divider lines in step 1, stitch along those and backtack, especially at the top of pocket

edges. Otherwise, use dressmaker's chalk or disappearing marker to draw lines where you want the compartments to be, and stitch, backtacking at the pocket edges. The widths of the compartments can vary (our roll has slots from 1¼" to 2¾" wide). Be sure to move the ribbon out of the way when you stitch (do not stitch it down).

ON A ROLL

To use the Artist's Roll, start by folding over the top by about 4". This will keep the items in the roll from falling out. Next, fold over about a third of the roll on the left, fold again on the right, and then tie with the ribbon.

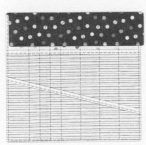 

Tool Holster

This holster is really a one-pocket tool belt. Modify it by changing the size of the pocket to hold another gadget or tool — or by adding additional pockets. For scissors, pruning shears, or anything sharp or pointy, you'll want a heavy-duty fabric so the tool won't poke through. For a waterproof version, make the holster with vinyl, laminated cotton, or oilcloth.

OUR FINISHED SIZE: 3½" × 7", two 31" belt ties

WHAT YOU'LL NEED

+ ½ yard of fabric for the holster and waist belt
+ 1 yard of ¼" double-fold bias tape
+ Sewing supplies (*see page* 18)

WHAT YOU'LL DO

+ Decide your size
+ Cut your fabric
+ Make the pocket
+ Make the holster back
+ Make and attach the belt ties
+ Attach the pocket

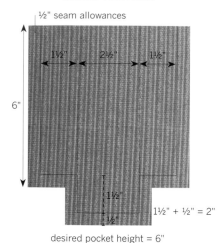

DECIDE YOUR SIZE

½" seam allowances

1½"   2½"   1½"

6"

1½"

1½" + ½" = 2"

½"

desired pocket height = 6"

CUT YOUR FABRIC

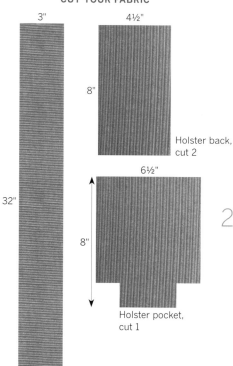

3"

4½"

8"

Holster back,
cut 2

6½"

8"

32"

Holster pocket,
cut 1

Belt, cut 2

Measure and Cut

1. **DECIDE YOUR SIZE.** What are you going to holster?
Your phone? Pruning shears? Whatever it is, lay
it on the fabric and measure it to determine the
size of the pocket. Be sure to include the depth in
your measurement and allow for ease (a little extra
room to get your tool in and out).

3-D POCKET PLANNING

To shape the pocket, think about how wide
and how deep the pocket needs to be and map
out the measurements as shown. Our finished
pocket is 1½" deep and 2½" wide at the front.
Don't forget to allow for ½" seam allowances.

BELT CONSIDERATIONS

Measure your waist (or hips, if you like to wear it
low) for your belt length (*see page* 15.). Be sure
to include plenty of extra inches for tying the
belt. You can always cut off what you don't need.
We cut our belt 3" wide for a finished width of 1".

2. **CUT YOUR FABRIC.** Draw the pieces on the wrong
side of the fabric and cut out the following:

+ *two holster back pieces*
+ *one holster pocket*
+ *two belt ties*

Put It Together

3. **MAKE THE POCKET.** Enclose the top raw edge of the pocket with bias tape and edgestitch. (*See page 46.*) Fold the fabric right sides together, matching the cut-out corner edges. Stitch to within ½" of outer edges and backtack, so the corners can be spread when stitched to the holster back.

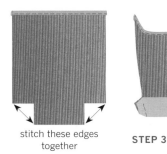

stitch these edges together

STEP 3

4. **MAKE THE HOLSTER BACK.** Pin the back pieces wrong sides together and round off all four corners. Stitch all the way around ½" from the edge, and trim the seam allowance to ¼".

5. **MAKE AND ATTACH THE BELT TIES.** Make the belt ties in the same way you'd make a strap. (*See page 42.*) Pin one end of each belt tie to one side of the holster back, as shown.

Holster back

STEP 4   **STEP 5**

6. **ATTACH THE POCKET.** Pin the pocket to the holster and stitch a ¼" seam around the edge, catching the belt ties as you stitch. Enclose the edge of the holster all the way around with double-fold bias tape (*see page 46*).

A BETTER ANGLE

To improve how the holster hangs, fold each belt tie as shown. Pin and test the angle until you have it the way you want it. Stitch two lines to hold the straps in place, backtacking for reinforcement.

STEP 6

A BETTER ANGLE

Caddy

This handy hanging caddy is great for organizing an entryway, craft space, or home office. With so many ways to customize the size, shape, and pockets, you'll have fun coming up with new designs for different uses. To hold bulkier small stuff, try adding a row of pleated pockets. Tie the caddy to the back of a chair or hang it up on some funky hooks. You decide!

OUR FINISHED SIZE: 17" × 14", four 10½" straps

WHAT YOU'LL NEED

+ ½–⅜ yard of fabric for the caddy body

+ ½ yard of fabric for the pockets

+ ⅛ yard of fabric for the ties

+ 1½ yards of ¼" or ½" double-fold bias tape (optional)

+ Sewing supplies (*see page* 18)

WHAT YOU'LL DO

+ Decide your size

+ Cut your fabric

+ Make the ties

+ Make the pockets

+ Stitch the sides

+ Add the ties and finish the top edge

15"

18"

Caddy body,
cut 2

11½"

2"

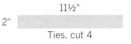

Ties, cut 4

7½"

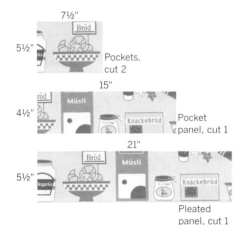

5½"

Brod

Pockets,
cut 2

15"

4½"

Müsli

Knäckebröd

Pocket
panel, cut 1

21"

5½"

Bröd   Müsli

Knäckebröd

Pleated
panel, cut 1

Measure and Cut

1. **DECIDE YOUR SIZE.** How much room do you have
to hang your caddy? How many pockets would
you like and what kind? We made three different
pocket styles on our caddy to show some variety.
You can choose one, two, or all three of these styles
to create the perfect configuration for your needs.

2. **CUT YOUR FABRIC.** Draw the pieces on the wrong
side of the fabric and cut out the following:

   + *two caddy body pieces*
   + *four tie strips (Note: Cut the strips wide enough
     to fold over and stitch the edges. For the caddy
     shown, we cut 2" wide strips.)*
   + *pockets or pocket panels, as desired*

   ### PLEATED POCKETS

   If you want to make pleated pockets, we'll tell
   you how in a minute. But how do you figure out
   how much fabric to cut? It's easy. Just add 2" to
   the width of each pleated pocket. Three pockets?
   Add 6" to the width. Don't forget to also add 1"
   for two ½" seam allowances.

Put It Together

3. **MAKE THE TIES.** Make the ties as you would make
straps (*see page 42*), and set them aside for now.

4. **MAKE THE INDIVIDUAL POCKETS.** Make pockets as instructed on pages 43–44. To finish pockets, you don't need to press under the top edge of the pocket — just enclose it with double-fold bias tape (the narrower fold on top) and edgestitch. (*See page* 46.)

5. **MAKE THE SIMPLE POCKET PANEL.** For a multipocket flat panel, like our middle row, first bind or hem the top edge as described in step 4. Press under the bottom edge ½". With right sides facing out, lay the panel on the front caddy piece where you'd like it to be. Stitch along the bottom of the panel to attach. Measure out desired sizes of pocket slots and stitch the dividing lines, backtacking at both ends. Machine-baste the pocket panel ¼" from both sides.

STEP 5

6. **MARK THE PLEATS.** To make the pleated panel, first attach bias tape to the top edge, as with the other pockets. Each pleat needs 1" of fabric, which will be folded in the middle, so plot out the stitching lines and fold lines as shown.

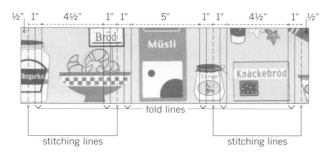

½" 1"   4½"   1" 1"   5"   1" 1"   4½"   1" ½"

fold lines

stitching lines   stitching lines

STEP 6

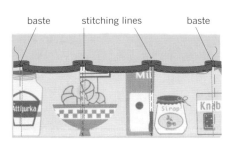

baste   stitching lines   baste

STEP 7

Caddy front

Caddy back

STEP 8

Caddy back

STEP 9

7. **ATTACH THE PLEATED PANEL.** With right sides facing out, place the pleated pocket panel on the front caddy piece, aligning the bottom edges. Press the folds of each pleat and stitch between the pockets on the stitching lines, backtacking at the top edge for reinforcement. Pin and machine-baste the pocket panel to the front of the caddy ¼" from the bottom and sides.

> **POCKET POSITION**
> If you are placing your pleated pockets somewhere other than the bottom edge of the caddy, you'd need to turn under the bottom edge of the panel and stitch it in place.

8. **STITCH THE SIDES.** With right sides together, pin and stitch the back caddy panel to the front caddy panel along the sides and bottom, leaving the top open. Clip the corners, trim the seam allowance, and turn the caddy right side out. Press under the top raw edges ½" and press.

9. **ADD THE TIES.** Place the ties side by side, in pairs, about 2" from sides of caddy. Insert the ends into top edge. Pin and topstitch along the top edge to secure the ties, and edgestitch close the top of caddy. If you plan to put heavy items in your caddy, you may want to double-stitch the top edge for reinforcement.

HANGING ON THE LINE

If you prefer, you can attach loops instead of ties. Just make a loop and stitch the ends into the caddy the same way you would the ties.

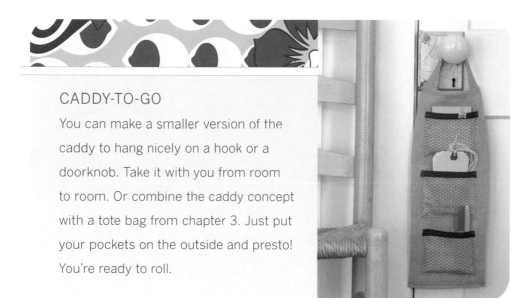

CADDY-TO-GO

You can make a smaller version of the caddy to hang nicely on a hook or a doorknob. Take it with you from room to room. Or combine the caddy concept with a tote bag from chapter 3. Just put your pockets on the outside and presto! You're ready to roll.

Resources

Periodicals

Creative Needle
800-443-3127
www.creativeneedlemag.com

Fiberarts
800-875-6208
www.fiberarts.com

Sew News
800-289-6397
www.sewnews.com

Sewing Savvy
800-449-0440
www.clotildessewingsavvy.com

Threads
Taunton Press
800-477-8727
www.taunton.com/threads

Sewing Machine Information

http://parts.singerco.com

http://sewing.about.com

www.sewing.org

www.sewingmanuals.net

www.sewusa.com

www.sewvac1.com/Library/tips.htm

www.tias.com/stores/relics

Fabrics, Notions & Tools

The best way to select fabric is hands-on. Check your yellow pages under "fabric shops" or "quilting" for local sources of fabrics, tools, and notions. You can also find all kinds of sewing supplies, tips, and ideas online at sites like these:

www.ciaspalette.com

www.craftyplanet.com

www.denverfabrics.com

www.ebay.com

www.gloriouscolor.com

www.hartsfabric.com

www.jandofabrics.com

www.mjtrim.com

www.sewzannesfabrics.com

www.sublimestitching.com

www.warmbiscuit.com

www.zandsfabrics.com

Index

METRIC CONVERSIONS

For those of you using metric measurements, here are some basic conversion formulas:

Multiply inches x 2.54 to get centimeters

Multiply feet x 0.305 to get meters

Multiply yards x 0.915 to get meters

Other Storey Titles You Will Enjoy

Colorful Stitchery, by Kristin Nicholas.
Dozens of embroidered projects to embellish and enhance any home.
208 pages. Paper. ISBN 978-1-58017-611-8.

Sew & Stow, by Betty Oppenheimer.
Out with plastic bags and in with 30 practical and stylish totes of all types!
192 pages. Paper. ISBN 978-1-60342-027-3.

Sew What! Fleece, by Carol Jessop & Chaila Sekora.
Thirty cozy projects in the perfect fabric choice for the Sew-What! woman — fleece.
160 pages. Hardcover with concealed wire-o. ISBN 978-1-58017-626-2.

Sew What! Skirts, by Francesca DenHartog & Carole Ann Camp.
A fast, straightforward method to sewing a variety of inspired skirts — without relying on store-bought patterns.
128 pages. Hardcover with concealed wire-o. ISBN 978-1-58017-625-5.

Uniquely Felt, by Christine White.
The essential and complete primer on feltmaking, from fulling and shaping to nuno and cobweb.
320 pages. Paper. ISBN 978-1-58017-673-6.

These and other books from Storey Publishing are available
wherever quality books are sold or by calling 1-800-441-5700.
Visit us at *www.storey.com.*